The Schools We Need

New Assumptions for Educational Reform

Arthur W. Combs

UNIVERSITY
PRESS OF
AMERICA

Lanham • New York • London

LA
217.2
.C66
1991

Copyright © 1991 by

University Press of America®, Inc.

4720 Boston Way
Lanham, Maryland 20706

3 Henrietta Street
London WC2E 8LU England

Library of Congress Cataloging-in-Publication Data

Combs, Arthur W. (Arthur Wright), 1912-
The schools we need : new assumptions for educational reform /
Arthur W. Combs.
p.   cm.
Includes index.
1. Educational change—United States.   I. Title.
LA217.2.C66   1991
370'.973—dc20   91-10001 CIP

ISBN 0–8191–8204–4 (alk. paper

 The paper used in this publication meets the minimum requirements of
American National Standard for Information Sciences—Permanence
of Paper for Printed Library Materials, ANSI Z39.48–1984.

To Susan, Lynn and Erin

TABLE OF CONTENTS

PREFACE

For several generations the problem of educational reform has been a matter of much concern to legislators, parents and to many in the educational profession itself. Most recently, the outcry for reform from every quarter has reached an all time high. From the current furor one might well infer that the matter has been totally neglected. As a matter of fact an enormous amount of energy has been devoted to the problem for many years with precious little to show for the effort. An enormous literature on the topic has accumulated. Thousands of solutions have been advocated and hundreds have been tried with disappointing results. Dedicated teachers and administrators have burned themselves out in the effort to make our schools more effective. Yet, despite all these attempts, our public schools fall farther and farther behind the expectations of our rapidly changing society.

As we enter the 90's the problem of education reform has reached a fever pitch. Public concern is about to redouble the pressure for change and the nation is preparing to throw new millions at the task with little hope of vitally changing the system. Four factors, especially, provide the basis for so dismal a prognosis. They are:

1. The failure to examine fundamental assumptions. Whatever plans we make for reform are inevitably controlled by the assumptions from which we begin. Plans made from the same erroneous or inappropriate assumptions can only result in inadequate solutions. They lock reformers into trying harder at the same old stands, doing more of what failed to work in the first place. Solutions based upon inappropriate assumptions produce reforms that fail to solve the basic problems. Worse still, they may produce token gains that only encourage more assiduous efforts based on the same tired hypotheses.

2. Failure to react to new expectations spawned by our rapidly changing modern world. A prime purpose of education is to prepare our youth for the future they will inherit. The educational system devised for the children of fifty years ago is no longer adequate for today's youth. It cannot prepare young people for the present, much less for the world they are about to enter. Goals for effective reform must be based upon the best understanding available about the nature and demands of the future.

3. Failure to incorporate and adapt to new discoveries about the nature of the human organism and how it learns and changes. For example, the past twenty years have seen astounding breakthroughs in our knowledge

about the human brain which require fundamental changes in our concepts of teaching and learning. The social sciences have provided similar breakthroughs about learning, behavior, the sense of self, health, ill health and the dynamics of human interrelationships, growth and intelligence. Many of these concepts are forty years old or more but have yet to be widely translated into educational thought and practice.

4. Failure to construct a system which values and facilitates innovation and true professionalism. Instead, we have created an enormous bureaucracy which stoutly maintains the status quo and treats its teachers as "delivery systems" or "cogs in the machine". Bureaucracies typically resist reform. No reform, of whatever variety, can hope to succeed without the consent and cooperation of the teachers who must carry it to fruition. A management oriented, top down approach to reform is inadequate to initiate or facilitate the reforms we so desperately need.

It is not my intent in this volume to write a how- to book for reform. We have had too much of that already. I do not believe effective reform can be successfully accomplished by top-down laid on solutions injected into the system without reference to basic assumptions or the persons expected to implement them. There is widespread agreement among education's critics that effective reform must come about from the bottom up as a consequence of:

1. Clear understanding of the problems confronted,

2. System wide grass roots involvement of the profession,

3. The creation and facilitation of alternative schools and programs, ·

4. Systematic attempts to implement new assumptions from modern science and research,

5. Fundamental changes in the job descriptions and training of teachers and administrators involved in the process.

I have been a teacher in public schools and colleges since 1935. During those years I have served the profession at various times as counselor, administrator, supervisor, teacher educator, researcher and consultant. Throughout that period I have also been deeply involved in formulating and interpreting perceptual-experiential psychology and its implications for educational thought and practice. As psychologist and educator, I have searched for ways to apply the best we know from the social sciences to achieve the goals of education. I have been an ardent innovator all my professional life. In the course of that experience I have acquired a profound admiration for and confidence in the capacity of teachers and administrators to tackle the problems of education and to arrive at ingenious solutions when they are given the freedom, trust and encouragement to do so. When teachers and administrators understand a problem and are free to explore it fully, they manage to arrive at remarkably sound and creative solutions. What is needed for effective reform is the release and encouragement of that enormous resource.

I hope this volume will contribute to that end. I have purposely avoided espousing specific methods and techniques for reform. I have done that intentionally, in part, because research clearly demonstrates that there are no universal right ones, and in part, because the application of methods or techniques without reference to basic assumptions is in large part responsible for the current mess we are in. Instead, I have tried:

a. to contribute a broader, deeper understanding of the problems we confront,

b. to set forth some new assumptions from modern social and scientific advances from which effective reform must begin, and

c. to outline some of the major implications they hold for educational thought and practice.

I am deeply indebted to the Association for Supervision and Curriculum Development for permission to reprint material from their publications, Humanistic Education: Objectives and Assessment and Perceiving, Behaving, Becoming: A New Focus For Education.

The ideas presented here have served me well as guidelines for my own attempts at innovation, program building and reform. I offer them in the hope that they may be equally helpful to colleagues in the profession, to citizens concerned about our schools and to parents concerned about the adequacy of their children's educational experience.

AWC

CHAPTER 1

WHY REFORMS HAVEN'T WORKED

Everyone thinks our educational system needs reform. Complaints are heard from every corner; from parents, the public, legislatures, Departments of Education, school boards, administrators, teachers, and the students themselves. In the face of this universal concern, why have we not made greater headway?

It isn't because we haven't tried. We've tried a hundred things. Here are just a few; the Palmer method, phonics, teaching machines, teacher aids, psychological testing, audio-visual equipment and techniques, open schools, open classrooms, team teaching, teacher aids, social promotion, the New Math and the New Science, languages in the early grades, tracking, homogeneous grouping, inquiry learning, behavior modification, reward and punishment, systems analysis, grades, competition and, most recently, behavioral objectives, competency based instruction, "back to the basics", computer technology and voucher systems. Each of these, in its time, was enthusiastically advanced as a solution to education's major ills. As it became evident that it, too, was as disappointing as its predecessors it was soon laid aside. Changing public education is like punching a pillow or, as someone has suggested, "Like moving a cemetery; after you've done all the work, you still have a cemetery"

Hundreds of reasons for our dilemma have been advocated. Some blame teachers, the teacher's colleges, the credential system or teacher unions. Others blame the government, inadequate budgets, working mothers, the breakdown of family and church, the moral decay of society, the insidious machinations of secular humanism, even the dire subversion of our youth by communism. Still others zero in on school programs; too much or not enough math, science, english, athletics, or sex education, lack of rigor in the classroom, frills in the curriculum or departures from the basics. The list is almost endless and much too complex to be of much help in formulating effective reforms.

Many of the criticisms raised by education's critics are valid concerns. Indeed, we are swamped with good ideas. Most of the reforms in the list above will improve learning somewhat when appropriately used. That is, when they are smoothly incorporated into a teacher's personal armamentarium of techniques on one hand and adapted to the overall curriculum and goals of a school on the other. Unfortunately, four overriding roadblocks to reform prevent that from happening. They are:

1. Failure to recognize the people problem.

2. Preoccupation with the manipulation of forces concept.

3. The problem of large schools.

4. Inhibition of the teaching profession.

Changing Education Is A People Problem

The reform attempts in the list above are not bad ideas. They are logical, rational proposals that ought to make things better. Why haven't they been more successful? A glance at the list on page one will make it clear that our efforts at reform have been preoccupied with "things". The things we have tried have been gadgets, gimmicks, legislative or administrative fiat, changes in methods, curricula, or ways of organizing and evaluating. All these efforts have missed the basic problem. Education is not a matter of things; it is a people problem.

At any moment our public education system involves about a hundred million persons including students, teachers, administrators and ancillary personnel. Such an enormous crowd of human beings cannot be changed by tinkering with things. It is people who must change, students, teachers, supervisors, administrators, school boards, parents. The system can only be deeply influenced through people, especially those on the firing line, the teachers. Unless we enlist teachers in the process of reform, whatever else we do will be of little avail.

It is a common phenomenon in dealing with institutions to concentrate attention on the persons at top and bottom while ignoring the one's in the middle. In hospitals, for example, we are concerned about the physicians, surgeons and the patients but overlook nurses, therapists, aids, teachers. In our penal institutions we are preoccupied with the warden and the prisoners and by pass the guards, teachers, counselors and ancillary personnel. Similarly, in education, we worry about the administration on one hand, and about the students on the other. Teachers, the people on whom the whole process depends, are given short shrift, or are ignored all together. Worse still, they are often blamed for most of our failures.

Laid On Solutions Rarely Work

Most of the attempts at reform mentioned on page one are laid on solutions. That is, they represent ideas, practices, ways of organizing or evaluating classroom activities not conceived by the persons who will have to utilize them. Most of those proposals were thought up by "experts", theorists, or administrators. With the best of intentions, they were introduced into the system by administrators or supervisors who, in turn, expected teachers to accept them as enthusiastically as those who contrived them.

A good example of this scenario can be found in the Behavioral Objectives effort of a few years back. This idea, taken over from industrial practice, went something like this: The systematic way to produce change is to---

1. Define your objectives clearly,
2. Construct a strategy to achieve them,
3. Gather the resources you need,
4. Put the plan into effect,
5. Then, assess how it worked out.

That plan looks efficient, logical, straightforward and business-like. Theoretically, it ought to produce excellent results. However, when the plan was laid on teachers, already loaded down with paperwork and extraneous expectations, it was often seen as just another frustrating interference imposed by the administration. Many teachers did not believe it was such a hot idea. Many more resented the additional burdens it placed upon an already difficult and demanding task. Still others decided to give it a half hearted effort and hope that it would go away like all previous attempts had done. Teachers met the plan with a wide variety of reactions; resignation, anger, annoyance, boredom, apathy, resistance, doubt or subversion, to name but a few. Almost no one, except for administrators and school boards, regarded it with enthusiasm. Accordingly, thousands of teachers all across the country turned in their required "Behavioral Objectives Plans" for the following week on Friday. Then, when they came to work on Monday, went right ahead with the things they always did. So, a "logical" idea died aborning because it did not take into account the people who would be expected to implement it. Logic is like that. Sometimes, logic is only a systematic way of arriving at the wrong answers.

It is time we recognized that changing education requires changing people. Changing things will never pull it off. Whatever we attempt must concentrate on producing change in the ways people think, work and affect each other in the person centered institution we call our public schools. Especially, we need to find ways of helping teachers find more adequate and satisfying ways of thinking and acting in their highly important and demanding occupations. Educational reforms which do not have whole-hearted support of those who must carry them out are a waste of time, effort and the taxpayer's money.

The Manipulation Of Forces Assumption

Education might have made greater headway in adapting to a changing population and an increasingly complex society had it not been saddled with an inadequate concept of motivation and behavior. American education has been in the grip of a "manipulation of forces" concept for dealing with human beings. The viewpoint holds that how people behave is a direct function of the forces exerted upon them. If that is so, it follows that motivation is the process of exerting forces on persons such as to cause them to do what the motivator has in mind. These two basic principles about human behavior have provided the guidelines for action at every level of our school system for several generations.

The manipulation of forces assumption about people and behavior seems simple and self evident. We see it in operation everywhere; at home, at work, on the playing fields. One can observe it affecting the behavior of the people around one. People do, indeed, seem to behave in response to the forces they confront. The assumption is also supported by physical science---things change when the forces exerted upon them change. For fifty years the manipulation of forces concept has also had the endorsement of psychologists who know it as behavioral psychology, stimulus-response psychology or behavior modification. In these theories behavior change is regarded as the result of stimuli to which a person is exposed or is confirmed by consequences following the behavior.

The manipulation of forces approach to changing behavior has been applied to all aspects of education. In the classroom it is widely accepted as the basic theory of learning. It is employed to develop the strategy and tactics of teaching, counseling, administration, classroom management and control. Teachers become tellers, demonstrators, rewarders and punishers of student performance. The primary tools of the trade are lectures, demonstrations, assignments, recitation, discipline and examination. Teachers attempt to change student behavior by advice, exhortation, modeling, praise, shame, competition, guilt or a thousand devices for conveying approval or disapproval. Sometimes these methods work to spur students to successful achievement. When techniques fail, however, no one questions the validity of the basic assumption. Instead, the reasons for failure are generally ascribed to not using methods well enough, often enough or with sufficient vigor and determination. That failing, blame can always be placed upon the intransigence of the student or parental mismanagement.

The manipulation of forces idea leads one to think that effective change can be brought about by managing the things to which people seem to be responding. Accordingly, legislatures attempt to influence education by controlling budgets, enrollment, curricula, or appropriating funds for research, plants or equipment. School boards and administrators carry the principle further as they formulate rules, regulations, memos or directives of a hundred varieties. The focus of reform is concentrated on management; the manipulation of things or persons toward desirable educational goals.

The Crucial Character Of Assumptions

Whatever people do in attempting to cope with problems they confront is dependent upon the assumptions from which they begin. Sound assumptions lead to effective solutions. Inaccurate ones produce inadequate results. When people believed the world was flat, they stayed away from the edge to avoid falling off. When we believed sickness was a consequence of bad blood, patients were bled, sometimes to death. When it was believed that children were only small sized adults, child labor was approved in order to prepare children to take on adult responsibilities.

The decisions we make about education in general or reform in particular are also dependent upon the assumptions from which we begin. The dilemma we currently face, however, is not from wrong assumptions. Wrong assumptions lead to disastrous results. Because disastrous outcomes are dramatic and inescapable, the assumptions that led to them are quickly given up. A much bigger problem exists when the assumptions from which we begin are partly right. There are perhaps no greater obstacles to human progress than partly right ideas. The trouble with partly right assumptions is that they get partly right results. Partially right outcomes, turn people's attention away from examining basic assumptions. Instead, they encourage us to keep on trying in the same directions in the vain hope that if we can only do the thing more often, with greater energy or more determination, in time we will achieve the success we so ardently hope for.

Our American education effort is saddled with dozens of partly right assumptions that impede our operations. Take the myth of competition, for example. It is generally believed that competition is an excellent means of motivating people. Accordingly, it is put to use everywhere in our society including our public schools. The assumption is only partly true. We know three things about competition: 1. The only people who are motivated by competition are those who believe they can win, 2. Persons forced to compete when they do not feel they have a chance of succeeding, are not motivated; they are discouraged and disillusioned, 3. When competition becomes too important, morality breaks down and any means becomes justified to achieve the ends. So the idea that competition is motivating is partly true---for those who think they can win. Nevertheless, the idea is widely and indiscriminately implemented overlooking the additional facts that competition is also discouraging and demoralizing.

A similar example can be found in the generally held belief that there are right methods of teaching. The fact is, despite thousands of researches on methods we are unable to isolate any method of teaching, counseling or administering which can be clearly shown to be associated with either good or bad performance. As a consequence we continue a fruitless search for right methods or apply those used successfully somewhere else to local students and curricula with negligible results. Educational thinking is hampered by dozens of inaccurate or outmoded assumptions. Many are myths of long duration.

Beginning from tired assumptions, we invent inadequate solutions. This keeps us trying more of what hasn't worked. It is time we recognized that many of our assumptions about reform are inadequate. "Sometimes you can sell more papers by shouting louder on the same corner. But, sometimes it is better to move to a new corner". It is time to search for new and more promising frames of reference for understanding the problem and finding better solutions.

The Importance Of Belief

The manipulation of forces assumption keeps obstructing the path of reform. The trouble with the manipulation of forces idea is not that it is wrong. Instead, it is partly right and that is what makes it so insidious. The problem lies in this; people don't behave directly in terms of the forces exerted upon them. They behave according to their <u>beliefs</u> about what is happening; and that can be very different from the way things look to an outside observer.

To understand the importance of beliefs in human behavior, we might draw an analogy with a giant computer. Complex modern computers take in enormous amounts of data from outside fed into the machine from a keyboard, tapes or cards. This information is stored in the computer's memory bank or combined with information already in the machine. The computer can then be used to solve all manner of problems when activated by a program. This is very much like what goes on in a human being. Each of us takes in great quantities of information from our experience of the worlds we live in. This information is combined with that already in our memory banks (brains?) and determines our behavior from moment to moment. What determines the behavior of the computer is the program employed to operate it. This is generally a set of mathematical or procedural instructions typed in by the operator. The behavior of persons is also determined by a program. Personal beliefs are the human programs. People behave or misbehave according to their beliefs or perceptions about themselves and the world. To change behavior it is necessary to change people's beliefs.

The Manipulation Of Forces Error

The trouble with the manipulation of forces idea is that it focuses on things rather than people. It also works for some matters. It works quite well, for example, when three conditions exist:

1. When goals to be achieved can be clearly defined

2. When goals are simple and uncomplicated,

3. When all of the controls are securely in the hands of the teacher or administrator.

Such highly specific conditions often occur in elementary classrooms, especially with respect to the teaching of simple techniques or skills. Applied to broader educational problems, the manipulation of forces idea is rarely sufficient. The activities required for modern educational reform almost never meet the above requirements. Instead, the goals of educational reform are often vague and ill defined. How shall we adapt the curriculum to individual student needs and capacities? How can we close the gap between the classroom and the community? How can we get people to see the need for a school bond issue? Even when goals can be clearly defined, they are rarely simple or uncomplicated. Quite the contrary. They tend to be broad and complex. Goals like good citizenship or mental and physical health, for example, don't lend themselves to detailed analysis or specific methods and techniques. Even quite specific goals like drug abuse or the drop out problem are enormously complex and require fundamental changes in the belief systems of parents, teachers and administrators to say nothing of changes in curricula and school practices.

Likewise, the means to achieve current goals in reform are rarely in the hands of the reformers. Instead, they require changes in thinking and behavior of thousands of persons, including students, teachers, supervisors, administrators, school boards, legislators and parents.

The goals of modern educational reform generally exist as complex problems to be solved, solutions to be found or generalized ends to be sought. To meet such objectives a different set of assumptions is required. If educational reform is, indeed, a people problem and if it is people's beliefs that determine their behavior, effective reform must be predicated upon the dynamics of changing people's beliefs. Fortunately, we have made great headway in recent years toward understanding that process. It is the purpose of this book to apply that knowledge to the problems of educational reform.

The Problem of Large Schools

As education became aware of the need to enrich its curriculum beyond the three R's, it increased the size of its schools so that classes in new or less popular subjects would d have a sufficient number of pupils to justify the expense of instruction. The trend has continued to the present. Schools with populations in the thousands can be found everywhere. Unfortunately, bigness creates pressure for commonality, depersonalization and conformity. Despite the notorious diversity of students, school systems continue to search for a common curriculum and ways to teach students as though they are alike.

Before we had public schools education was only available to those few who could afford it. The curriculum was comparatively restricted, confined for the most part to the traditional Three R's; reading writing and arithmetic. School attendance was regarded as a privilege and it was sink or swim for the students. Nobody worried about those who did not fit. They were summarily tossed out. The advent of public education meant all that had to change. With the admission of the great unwashed public it was no longer enough to fit the student to a limited curriculum; it became necessary to adapt the curriculum to the nature and needs of the student. If you are going to educate everyone, a richer curriculum is also required because students are notoriously different. Fitting the curriculum to the student calls for individualizing instruction.

This fundamental change in the task of schools became necessary almost 200 years ago and we are still struggling to find ways to bring it about. In a world of unique human beings and an ever expanding mountain of information the problem of helping children by the millions to grow as individuals continues to stump us. Though we advocate individualizing instruction we still have not figured out how to do it. Instead, we spend enormous energy trying to find ways to avoid confronting the issue. Schools are commonly structured in grade levels, homogeneous grouping or tracking systems. Teaching is directed to the average student leaving faster or slower learners to adapt as best they can. We search for ways to ignore student diversity and organize our classrooms to deal with young people as though they were alike.

We search for a common curriculum applicable to the largest possible numbers. Whole industries have been spawned to take advantage of the need for common textbooks, workbooks, curricular and teaching materials. It is a lucrative business running to billions of dollars. In turn, schools and teachers become seduced into reliance upon such materials thus producing boredom for themselves and squelching the creativity of students. As Donald Snygg once commented, "The trouble with American education is that we are all trying desperately to give students answers to problems they don't have yet!" To which we might add, "and may never have".

A System Out Of Touch With Its Consumers

Bigness and commonality has at least three insidious and destructive effects. For one, they create a system increasingly out of touch with its consumers. The trend to larger and larger schools has produced a system in which students are treated, almost literally, as cogs in a great machine while teachers are frequently referred to as "delivery systems". Students get lost in large schools. No one knows who they are. Personal contact with teachers is reduced almost to zero. Students and teachers become adversaries. At the high school level students bitterly complain that the system is irrelevant to their needs. Many elect to drop out. Younger students do not have the luxury of that option and must cope with the system as best they can. As Earl Kelley often remarked, "We have these marvelous schools, great teachers, magnificent curricula and equipment. Then, Damn it all! The parents send us the wrong kids!". Bigness may make it possible to teach a greater diversity of courses. It also creates problems so insidious and far reaching as to seriously interfere with truly effective teaching and learning.

I once asked a class of young teachers-in-training, "How come students don't get involved?" Here are some of the things they told me:
Nobody believes what we think is important.
Nobody trusts us.
All schools want is conformity.
They feed us a Pablum diet--its all chewed over.
They are afraid to let us try.
Nobody cares.
Teachers and students are enemies--they should be friends.
It's details, details, details.
Everyone worries about grades--as though they mattered.
You can't question anything.
The only good ideas are the old ones--what's in the books.

The discussion closed on this shocker, which everyone agreed was true: "The things worth getting committed to don't get you ahead in school"! Seen from the student's perspective, school is a place that deals with things that don't really matter.

Lack Of Adjustment To Changing Needs

A second inhibiting effect of bigness and commonality is the lack of response to changing needs. Bigness and commonality produce a bureaucracy with stubborn resistance to change. A major source of our current problems lies in the failure of schools to adapt sufficiently to a changing world. Despite enormous changes in the world we inhabit, we continue to operate on out of date assumptions no longer appropriate for the times, the students or the problems we have to confront. Reliance upon mass produced textbooks and materials only contributes further to this inertia.

Discouraging Innovation

A third effect of bigness is to place a damper upon innovation. Innovation requires breaking out of the mold, doing something different. Unhappily, bigness and the need for commonality make effective innovation uphill work. Experimentation is often discouraged before it gets started. Innovators are regarded with suspicion for "rocking the boat." The system encourages conformity, the antithesis of creativity. If you want people to conform they are unlikely to be creative. If you want them to be creative, you can count on it, they will not be likely to conform. The history of educational innovation is replete with examples of fine programs placed in operation, then destroyed or abandoned by opposition or neglect. In his book, Freedom To Learn For The 80s, Carl Rogers cited a dozen or more excellent programs which bloomed for a short term then quietly died, done in by too much success.

Educators everywhere suffer from a pathological fear of mistakes. The system is built on right answers. Everywhere a premium is placed on being right. That is what testing pays off on and grading systems or school accreditations display to public view. As a consequence, everyone is fearful of making mistakes, students, teachers, administrators. Everyone seeks to play it safe. Field trips are avoided because someone might get hurt. Teachers and administrators are scared to death of parents who might complain about what they do. Inhibiting rules and regulations are formulated to cover every conceivable eventuality. Risk taking is discouraged at every turn. Unhappily, such attitudes destroy teacher interest in innovation and reform.

The Industrial Model

To deal with larger schools, administrators have turned to industry in search of management models. School boards and school administrators everywhere have adopted various forms of the industrial model for public education. They still do. Whenever industrial planners develop a new management fad it is quickly adopted by hundreds of school administrators as well. This infatuation with the methods of industry creates additional problems for educational reform.

The application of the industrial model depersonalizes the system and sidetracks innovation. The industrial model is simply inappropriate for the educational endeavor. For industry, the worker is part of the machinery required for the production of industry's product. In education, <u>the worker is the product</u>. This is a crucial distinction. If industry were organized for the welfare of the worker, instead of the production of a product, it would not be organized the way it is. Preoccupation with the industrial model creates a serious roadblock to thinking, practice and innovation. An institution like education, primarily organized for the   growth and fulfillment of its participants needs a structure specifically designed for that end.

Inhibiting The Profession

One of the saddest outcomes of the manipulation of forces assumption is the insidious erosion of the teaching profession it has brought about. All occupations require knowledge and skills relative to their fields of expertise. What generally distinguishes a profession from other forms of work is the degree of complexity of the task involved and heavy reliance upon the problem solving capacities of the professional practitioner. A major characteristic of the teaching profession is its dependence upon immediate response. When a child says something, the teacher must reply. When something happens the teacher must deal with the event; not tomorrow or after he/she has looked up the answer, but right now. This means that teachers must be skilled at confronting problems and coming up with immediate solutions. To do that effectively requires problem solving abilities of a high order. It also requires a can-do attitude of respect for self and one's profession.

The areas in which teachers are free to utilize their professional skills are strictly limited to the classroom. Even that theater of operations is filled with all manner of constraints imposed by the school organization, the curriculum, administration, faculty, school or parental expectations, time or equipment. Rarely do teachers have opportunity to participate outside the classroom in decisions about policy, curriculum, standards, organization, assessment or long term planning. Small wonder that many teachers suffer from low self esteem. In addition, teachers are confronted with wide spread devaluation of the profession by the public which generally believes that, "People who can, do. People who can't, teach and people who can't teach, teach teachers".

As low man on the totem pole teachers are often looked upon as lightweights from whom little can be expected. Their professional training is denigrated by demands that teachers colleges increase requirements for subject matter and reduce requirements for so called professional study. There is even a lively movement afoot to by pass professional training entirely and to recruit into the profession persons exclusively trained in subject matter.

It is characteristic of democracy to expect public servants to do their jobs, always reserving the right to "kick like the devil" when one suspects they are not. Accordingly, teachers are rarely praised or rewarded for the things they do well but hear about it "loud and clear" when the public is dissatisfied. Low regard for the profession seriously undermines teacher self esteem, contributes to burn out and discourages interest in reform.

An Exhausting Occupation

Contrary to public belief, teaching well done is a highly exhausting occupation. The task is complicated by an inordinate amount of busy work having little reference to educational goals. Except at the college level, schools allow minimum time for planning. Yet, teachers at the elementary level are expected to teach 25 to 35 students a day in ten or eleven subjects. At the high school level they work with 100 to 300 students a day in one to five subjects often with less than an hour of preparation. In the face of such demands it is not surprising that thousands of teachers slip into patterns of repetition, reliance upon canned curricula, audio-visual fill-ins, last year's plans or assorted forms of busy work as a matter of survival. When you are moving as fast as you can just to stand still, requests for change or orders to do more are bound to be met with resistance, if not anger, resentment or sabotage.

Like everyone else, teachers share the pathological fear of mistakes characteristic of the profession. As a consequence, they are hesitant to engage in professional dialogue or common projects. One would think that a profession so dependent upon human interaction would be deeply involved with colleagues. As a matter of fact, the profession is extraordinarily lonely. Teachers are fearful of being observed and rarely dialogue with others in the profession about matters beyond the mundane. Ask a plumber's permission to watch him plumb and he replies, "Sure, when would you like?" Ask a teacher a similar question and expect to get embarrassment, confusion and quickly discovered reasons why a visit would be disappointing. "You really wouldn't be interested". "I'm giving a test that hour" etc. etc.

Innovative teachers find themselves working against the grain. Departures from the expected are generally met with all sorts of objections from administrators and other teachers. Innovations cause trouble. They are disruptive. They make more headaches. Besides, they may not work. What then? It takes a courageous and committed teacher to venture out on a limb to propose an innovation outside his/her own classroom.

The Need For Grass-roots Innovation

Despite the low opinion of the profession and the innumerable roadblocks placed in the path of innovation, a remarkable number of high quality teachers manage to teach exceptionally well. The fact that our schools have done as well as they have is a tribute to the fundamental integrity and good faith of thousands of hard working, unappreciated teachers. Many find ways to change and adapt to the needs of students and the profession in highly promising ways. Some even manage to do this while working under the baleful eye of a pompous and autocratic administrator.

In the final analysis, it is teachers upon whom we must rely to implement reforms. Without their goodwill and cooperation, even the most promising reforms are doomed to failure. To bring about the reforms we so desperately need, it will be necessary to appreciate and recognize the teaching profession. It will also be necessary to recognize the vital role of teachers in the reform process; not only in implementation of reforms but in their invention as well. In short, teacher cooperation and input must be sought for every phase of the reform effort including the making of critical decisions. Anything less will simply perpetuate the sorry record of past attempts.

The Task Before Us

To reverse the unhappy trends of the past forty years many concerned citizens and educators are convinced that we need a fundamental restructuring of our public schools. We must find new ways to approach the problems of educational reform. John Chubb of the Brookings Institute and Terry Moe of Stanford University, for example, point out that, "school performance is simply unrelated to per pupil spending, teacher salaries, class size and graduation requirements". As a result of ten years of study involving 500 schools and 20,000 educators, they conclude that factors contributing to an effective school are a clear sense of purpose, strong leadership, highly professional teachers and high expectations of students. (Chubb, 1990). The authors maintain that only "bottom up accountability" can bring about the kinds of reforms we so desperately need. Such conclusions are shared by many other critics on the current scene including the national presidents of

14

both professional education organizations, Shanker, of the American Federation of Teachers and Futrell, of the National Education Association (Shanker, 1990, Futrell, 1989).

In this volume we will examine some of the assumptions required for a bottom up approach to educational reform with special attention to:

1. The changing goals of education in the 90's.

2. New knowledge about the nature of learning and behavior change.

3. The need for open system thinking.

4. The dynamics of change.

5. Alternative programs and alternative schools.

6. Basic requirements for a revitalized profession.

7. A new conception of leadership and administration.

Notes And References

General references:

Berliner, D. 1987 Contemporary teacher education: Timidity, lack of vision and ignorance. Paper, American Academy Of Education, Washington, D.C.

Boyer, E. 1983 High school: A report on secondary education in America The Carnegie Foundation for the Advancement of Teaching. New York, Harper and Row.

Coleman, J. 1966 Equality of Educational Opportunity Washington, D.C. Government Printing Office.

Eisner, E. 1985 What high schools are like: Views from the inside. Palo Alto, Stanford University Press.

Goodlad, J. 1983 A place called school. New York, McGraw Hill.

Kerr, S. 1989 "Reform in Soviet and American education: Parallels and contrasts" Phi Delta Kappan, 71,19-28.

National Commission on Excellence in Education, 1983, <u>A nation at risk: the imperative for educational reform</u>, Washington, D.C. Government Printing Office.

Ravitch,D. 1981 "Forgetting the question: The problem of educational reform", Summer, <u>The American Scholar</u>.

On the Manipulation of Forces Assumption:

Macmillan, D. 1973 <u>Behavior modification in education</u> New York, Macmillan.

Pitts, C. 1971 <u>Operant conditioning in the classroom</u>, New York, Crowell.

Skinner, B. 1971 <u>Beyond freedom and dignity</u>, New York, Alfred Knopf.

Sulzer, B. and Mayer, G. 1972. <u>Behavior modification procedures for school personnel</u>, Hinsdale, Il. Dryden Press.

On changing assumptions:

Combs, A. 1988 "Changing our assumptions about educational reform", <u>Educational Digest</u>, 54,3-7.

On myths in education:

Combs, A. 1957 "The myth of competition", <u>Childhood Education</u>,33,264-269.

Combs, A. 1979 <u>Myths in Education: Beliefs that hinder progress and their alternatives</u>, Boston, Allyn and Bacon.

Combs, A. 1979. "The myth of competition--Twenty years later" <u>Colorado Journal of Educational Research</u>, 18,5-7.

Johnson,D. and Johnson,R. 1975. <u>Learning together and alone.</u> Englewood Cliffs, N.J., Prentice Hall.

On some failed attempts at reform:

Rogers, C. 1983. <u>Freedom to learn for the 8o's</u>, Columbus, Oh. Merrill.

16

On the industrial model:

McDonald,J. 1989. "When outsiders try to change schools from the inside" Phi Delta Kappan,71,206-212.

Orlich,D. 1989. "Educational reform: Mistakes, misconceptions, miscues." Phi Delta Kappan, 71, 512-517.

On new directions for reform:

Chubb, J. and Moe, T. 1990. Politics, markets and America's schools Washington, D.C. The Brookings Institution.

Futrell, M. 1989. "Mission not accomplished: Educational reform in retrospect". Phi Delta Kappan, 71, 8-14.

Shanker, A. !990. "The end of the traditional model of schooling---and a proposal for using incentives to restructure our public schools". Phi Delta Kappan, 71,344-358.

Shanker, A. 1990. "On restructuring schools: A conversation with Al Shanker" Educational Leadership, 47,11-16.

CHAPTER 2

WHAT DO WE WANT OF OUR SCHOOLS ?

No modern society can afford to let its youth grow up without an education. An educational system is one of society's ways of perpetuating its existence. Some educational reformers have suggested that we ought to use our public schools to construct a new social order. That goal is unlikely to get very far because no society is apt to tolerate for long attempts by one of its institutions to overthrow the society. Schools that depart very far from society's fundamental purposes are not likely to be supported or indulged for very long. This means that educational reform is essentially a catch up operation rather than a pioneer activity. If that fact seems disappointing, it need not. Our current system will have all it can do for years to come just to come abreast of current needs. Before plunging into the strategy for reform, let us pause to explore some of the things we want of our schools.

Traditional Goals

Society's primary purpose in establishing schools is to assure the production of intelligent, responsible citizens who can be counted upon to protect and advance the welfare of society. To that end Americans have stated and restated their goals for education for 250 years. A comprehensive review of these objectives from the very beginning of public schools down to the latest national conferences on education boils down to seven "cardinal principles" which parents, scholars, educators and public officials have advocated repeatedly down the years.

1. Command of the fundamental processes and skills for effective learning. More specifically, this objective refers to the "three R's" of reading, writing and arithmetic. It is the most obvious of the objectives and lends itself most readily to simple straightforward assessment. For those reasons it always comes under heavy fire whenever people become alarmed about our schools. See, for example, the "back to the basics" movement of the last few years.

2. Preparation for worthy home membership. Though repeatedly included for generations, this objective has rarely been spelled out in the form of a specific curriculum.

3. Education for responsible citizenship. This is society's central objective, the primary purpose for which it supports education. All other

objectives contribute in one way or another to preparing youth to be effective citizens. The objective is more specifically sought through subjects like civics, social studies and history.

4. Mental and physical health. Physical health has been a long time objective. In more recent years we have added mental health to the category but we have made only marginal progress toward implementing it in either practice or the curriculum.

5. Basic skills for taking one's place in the world of work. This objective has become more and more important as our society has become increasingly industrialized. Some critics complain that we have gone too far toward making our educational system a prep school for the work place. On the other hand, employers complain that today's graduates are woefully unprepared to take their places in modern industry.

6. Education for effective use of leisure time. This category includes the arts, drama, music and literature. Unfortunately, it is also one of the most vulnerable when schools are faced with a budget crunch. It must fight for its life in competition with more "practical" objectives.

7. Education for moral and ethical character. This was a primary objective for the establishment of the earliest schools. With the flowering of our materialistic industrial society it lost some of its early urgency. For a time it came under attack from fundamentalist groups who saw it as a usurpation of the prerogatives of home and church. More recently, we have seen a resurgence of interest in values as a legitimate part of the curriculum.

More Immediate Goals

In addition to the general purpose of preparing intelligent, responsible citizens, communities use their schools for a variety of more immediate purposes. In recent years we have seen our public schools used as a vehicle to correct the social ills of segregation and racial prejudice. Some states seek to indoctrinate democratic ideals. They require courses in "Democracy vs. Communism" or the study of a state's peculiar history. In some communities schools are valued as agencies for keeping youth off the streets or out of the job market. Others use their schools to deal with specific problems like driver education, sex education, alcohol and drug abuse. Some school districts place high priorities on a winning athletic program.

Of course, our educational system cannot accept sole responsibility for any or all of these objectives. Critical influences upon young people are exerted by many other forces in our society; parents, peer groups, churches, community resources, to name but a few. That fact does not permit us to wash our hands of the matter, however. Schools must contribute whatever they can to meeting the goals society sets for its youth.

We Ask Ever More Of Our Schools

Changing patterns of family structure are laying a heavier and heavier burden upon our schools. We can no longer count upon stable family relationships for the teaching of fundamental values. Divorce and single parenting are commonplace. Mothers are joining the work force in ever larger numbers. With changes in the family come greater demands for education to fill the gaps. Much as one may deplore these changes in our society, the trends are unlikely to be reversed. Some institution must provide the security, knowledge, skills and understanding formerly acquired in the day to day interactions of the traditional family. Our public schools are the most obvious and available choice.

The influence of religion and the church is likewise declining in our modern industrial society. With lessening influence of these venerable institutions, we look to our schools to pick up the slack. A few years ago fundamentalist preachers were railing against "values clarification" in public schools. They branded the teaching of values as arrogant assumptions of the age old prerogatives of family and church. Today, they are often heard demanding that schools give greater attention to values education. We continue to expect our schools to assume responsibilities formerly ascribed to home and church. Nor is this likely to change in the foreseeable future. From all the observable signs we can only conclude these trends will continue.

As if this were not enough, public schools are confronted with ever larger numbers of children from diverse ethnic, racial and cultural origins. We are no longer a white, anglo-saxon, protestant nation. We are becoming ever more cosmopolitan. Immigration, desegregation, civil rights and a growing multicultural population place new demands upon our schools for the preparation of responsible citizens. The problem of individualizing instruction so that every child achieves the maximum of her capacities is a noble but increasingly difficult objective.

A More Complex Society

The world for which we were preparing children a hundred and fifty years ago was a far simpler place than the world we live in today. Our industrial-technological society is enormously complex and grows ever more so with each new scientific discovery. Once it was possible to take one's car apart and put it back together. But, who would be so foolish as to try that today? We are thoroughly dependent upon high tech gadgets and we have been forced to invent a whole new class of workers just to keep them operating. We must rely upon thousands of persons we have never seen or heard of for satisfaction of such simple needs as a loaf of bread or a carton of milk. To get some idea of the extent of our dependence upon others, one need but stand before the gleaming racks of a modern supermarket and think about all the people it took to get those things there for our use.

We live in the most interdependent, cooperative society the world has ever know since the dawn of human history. Our interdependence has also made us infinitely more vulnerable. The modern epidemic of terrorism is a product of this interdependence. One person in the right place at the right time can throw us all into panic by holding a hostage, shooting a president, crashing a plane, programming a computer or disrupting communication. Our technological society makes ever greater demands on the knowledge, skill and intelligence of its workers. Science and industry continually upgrade their expectations of schools and colleges. The task of educating youth to participate successfully in such a world is a far more difficult task than heretofore. If schools are to meet the minimum demands of today's society, drastic change is necessary. Tinkering is not enough.

Some Demands Imposed By What We Know Of The Future

The need for reform becomes even greater as we look to the future. We count on our schools to help prepare youth for the world into which they will be moving. To meet that objective it is necessary to have some conception of what the future is apt to be like. Futurists tell us we are living in the midst of a profound revolution that most people are not aware exists. The futures predicted for us are not wild dreams or science fiction. They are hard realities already upon us. While no one can predict with accuracy the precise nature of the world we are entering, futurists are generally agreed upon at least four certainties:

1.The Knowledge Explosion

The knowledge explosion we are currently experiencing will continue into the future expanding at exponential rates. We are awash in information and it continues to flow from every source in greater and greater volume. Once, teachers were among the best informed persons in town. Those days are gone forever. The idea of the teacher as fountainhead of knowledge is dead as a dodo. Science has provided us with marvelous techniques for the dissemination of information; radio, audio-visual equipment, copying machines, television, computers, recordings, libraries etc. These devices are capable of placing vast amounts of information in the hands of almost anyone quickly and efficiently. They have also made the teacher as information provider obsolete.

2.The Pace Of Change

The present is changing and the future will continue to do so at ever increasing speed. Most of the scientists who have ever lived are alive today. New ideas and inventions are commonplace. They occur so often that we have come to expect and depend upon them even as they change our very way of living. The stability we once could count upon is no longer a fact of life. We now have some 90,000 occupations and the number continues to climb. Students coming out of high school today may have to change their life work four or five times in their lifetimes. Preparation of youth for a world of such rapid change must surely be quite different from that of a stable, predictable society.

3.The Primacy Of People Problems

The complex, interdependent societies of the future will make people issues paramount. Already human problems have become the most pressing ones we face; global communication, war and peace, health and fitness, poverty and wealth, pollution and the environment, social security, child care, overpopulation, starvation, civil rights, women's lib, ethnic and racial discrimination, cultural diversity, drug, child and family abuse. Even the atomic bomb is a human problem. It is not the bomb we need fear but the people who might use it. The world continues to shrink. Just a short time back the United States and American products were far in the lead of other nations. Most recently, we have become a debtor nation increasingly dependent for manufactured goods on foreign countries and forced to compete in a global market. Every technological advance we make brings people closer together and imposes the necessity for learning how to live with many more. Understanding human relationships has become a survival skill. It is an essential for effective living in the world our youth will inhabit. Business as usual will not do. Preparation for that increasingly human oriented world must be a prime objective of our public schools.

4.Personal Fulfillment

More than ever, societies of the future will be dependent upon caring, responsible citizens, willing and able to pull their own weight. That calls for healthy human beings, persons who feel positively about themselves and sufficiently successful in fulfilling their personal needs to be responsive to the needs of others. Persons who feel negatively about themselves, frustrated and alienated from society are a danger to everyone. The personal fulfillment of citizens in an interdependent society is a necessary ingredient for society's continuing safety and welfare. The more we succeed in helping people achieve the satisfaction of basic needs, the more they are freed to seek the fulfillment of personal goals and aspirations. The principle is equally true for education. Students are more strongly motivated, committed and successful when their personal needs are essentially met. Even if educational and societal outcomes were not important we would still need to seek personal fulfillment as an educational objective on purely humanitarian grounds because we love our youth.

Some Implications For Education

The four certainties about the future just above have important implications for educational reform. Among those implications are the following:

1. <u>We can never again hope to design a curriculum to be required of everyone.</u> A common curriculum is no longer a tenable goal for education or reform. The quantity of available information is so great, change is so rapid and the future needs of students are so diverse that it is impossible to be sure that any specific subject matter will be essential. Reading, writing and arithmetic at least to the fifth grade level will probably remain essential goals for some time to come. Beyond those basic objectives how shall we determine what else must be pursued by all? The best we can hope for is to provide a curriculum responsive to student needs and aspirations within the limits of our financial and environmental resources. That will require a creative faculty, sensitive to the needs of youth, skilled in the adaptation of curricula to changing times and maximally free to apply their talents professionally.

2. <u>Intelligent persons---new goal for education.</u> An educational system unable to predict the specific knowledge or behaviors required for the future will have to concentrate its efforts on producing persons who are effective problem solvers. Tomorrow's citizens must be able to confront problems, marshall likely options and choose solutions on the spot. Unable to design a specific curriculum for the future, schooling must be directed to the production of intelligent persons. To achieve that end will require intensive concentration upon the growth and development of students, rather than content and subject matter. This calls for a more person-centered system than heretofore.

3. <u>Process oriented education.</u> Effective problem solving is learned by confronting events, defining problems, making choices, experimenting, trying,

searching for solutions. It is using your brain and all the resources you can command in the search for answers. Learning how to learn is more important than learning any given subject matter. Effective problem solving is a creative process not tied to any subject. It is also best learned from confrontation with real problems, not artificial ones. Research shows that students are most likely to be motivated when problems are real and personally relevant, when solutions seem within their capacities and when results are immediately discernible. Most current curricula would have great difficulty meeting those criteria. To provide students with real problems schools must open their doors to the community. Community resources must be invited into the classroom and students must be actively involved in the community. Local, state, national and international issues must become a significant part of the curriculum.

4. A future of change calls for life long learning The idea of "completing your education" at any age or finite period is obsolete for the world our youth will be entering. To cope with rapid change, education for the future must be lifelong. Already our society has made great headway in providing continuous educational opportunities for persons of all ages and interests. Our public schools must prepare youth to use these and other resources as often and as long as necessary. To meet that objective calls for positive attitudes toward learning. Students who become turned off by their school experience must be regarded as major failures of the system. Students must leave public schools equipped with the necessary skills for continued learning and the expectation that they will need to use them throughout their lives.

An interesting corollary of the life long learning principle is this: We are relieved of the pressure for students to "finish your education" at any particular time. Learners can enter or leave the system as often as necessary to meet their current or future needs. If citizens will be able to return to learning at any time, furthermore, there is no compelling need to hold reluctant learners in the system against their will. This opens the door for many new alternatives in our attempts to solve the high school drop out problem.

5.Concentration on the human condition. To prepare youth for a future in which human problems are primary, current curricula must concentrate far more on the human condition. We are moving from the era of physical science to the era of social science. The disciplines of psychology, sociology, anthropology and political science were invented to help us understand the nature of human beings and their interactions with one another. Those sciences are now over a hundred years old but are still not part of the curriculum of most schools, except occasionally, at the high school level as an elective for seniors. Understanding human beings and their relationships is no frill. It is a vital necessity for the world our youth will inhabit. Contributions to that end must become an integral part of the curriculum for all students beginning in nursery school.

Exploration of human relationships is not an esoteric subject reserved for upper level study. Even very young children are constantly engaged in relationships and the problems that entails. All students can utilize their own interrelationships as raw material for wider understanding of human beings and what makes them tick. Every community provides real life laboratories for the observation and study of all manner of human and social concerns.

6. Personal identity and fulfillment. If the search for personal fulfillment will be a major characteristic of the future, today's schools must accept the challenge and begin serious preparation for those ends. The fulfillment of personal needs is not "self Indulgence" as too many suppose. It is a necessary step to higher levels of motivation, achievement and responsible citizenship. The fulfillment of personal needs frees people to work for higher objectives. The genius of good teaching lies in helping students to fulfill their personal needs and to discover needs they never knew they had. The search for personal identity is widely recognized on a theoretical level as a developmental task for middle school and high school pupils. Knowledge of this vital stage in student growth has had little impact, however, on the goals and practices of most current schools. The matter is given little more than lip service in most places. Meanwhile students continue to complain that school is largely irrelevant, having little to do with the world as they know it. Far too many find their experience so unrewarding that they drop out of the system physically or mentally.

7. Education for social interaction and responsibility. The increasingly interrelated society of the future can only operate successfully if citizens can be counted upon to pull their own weight and look out for their fellows. Schools preparing youth for that world must emphasize responsibility and effective human relationships. Preoccupation with traditional subject matter can defeat those goals. Responsibility is learned from being given responsibility, never by having it withheld. It is learned like any other subject from successful experiences at simple levels followed by increasingly difficult problems paced to student readiness and capacities. Learning responsibility requires confronting problems, making choices, being involved in decisions, accepting the consequences of one's actions, learning from mistakes---not with artificial problems but real ones. Sensitivity and caring for others can also be learned from student's interactions with one another during the school years. All that is required is a shift in priorities from preoccupation with subject matter to increased concern for students as people. Teachers

with knowledge and skills for facilitating student growth and interactions can contribute greatly toward helping students acquire the understanding of themselves and others necessary for effective and happy citizenship.

8. Schools as microcosms. One would think it self evident that schools in a democratic society would model the cherished beliefs of such a society. Unhappily the atmospheres and organization of many of our schools are more akin to autocratic societies. Learning to live and work in a democratic atmosphere ought to be a high priority. In a world where human problems and responsible interactions are essential, schools must, themselves, become microcosms of democracy in action. People are scripted by their experience. They learn far more from personal experience than from any amount of subject matter. Concern for individuals, respect for human dignity and integrity, cooperative effort, respect for human rights, caring for others, must serve as guidelines, for the treatment of students and for the function and organization of schools as well. To prepare for a future dependent upon successful human interaction calls for schools that confront students daily with significant human problems, where students and faculty are continuously exploring effective interrelationships, where humane goals have high priority and all school personnel are actively seeking to model good human relationships.

New Insights From Science

To achieve the updated, self renewing schools we need requires more than adaptations to the changing needs of society and individual students. It requires, also, the incorporation of new discoveries from the physical and social sciences. The past thirty to forty years have brought fundamental scientific advances in two area of vital importance for education; new understandings from brain research and from perceptual- experiential psychologies. From each of these sources we have new information of such importance as to rival the breakthroughs in physical science. The insights they provide corroborate each other and call for major changes in thinking and practice about the nature of motivation and learning, the development of intelligence and personality, the nature of health and illness and the dynamics of human interrelationships. Whenever our beliefs about the nature of people, learning and human fulfillment change, the consequences extend into every aspect of our lives, especially for thinking and practice in education. These vital new discoveries provide yardsticks against which we can measure existing practices, suggest new parameters for reform and point to new ways for their effective implementation.

Brain Research

Recent research on brain functioning has provided us with a whole new understanding of that mysterious organ and how it works. We are told the brain is not merely a receiver and storehouse of information. Neither is it simply a processor and manipulator of information like a computer. Instead, it is far more remarkable and creative. We learn that the brain is a marvelous organ for the discovery and processing of meaning. It is constantly engaged in making sense out of experience. It does this by seeking patterns, relationships or approximations. This understanding calls for a new approach to teaching and learning. It means that learning must be defined as the discovery of meaning while teaching becomes the facilitation of that process.

Traditionally schools have regarded learning as the acquisition of knowledge, habits or skills and teaching as the manipulation of stimuli and consequences to those ends. Leslie Hart, in his book, <u>Human Brain and Human Learning</u>, (Hart 1983), points out that such assumptions about teaching and learning results in schools and classrooms at odds with what we now know of the brain and its operations. He is sharply critical of much in customary educational practice and calls for more "brain compatible" schools. To that end he has developed a theory of learning based upon modern brain research and has seen it implemented in several school systems with highly promising results.

Hart also discusses the negative or inhibiting effects of threat upon brain function. When people feel threatened or overwhelmed by experience, the brain "downshifts" from higher thought processes in the cerebrum to avoidance or defensive postures characteristic of older portions of the brain. He points to numerous practices in today's schools which tend to overwhelm or threaten learners and so make schools brain incompatible. He suggests a number of alternatives in atmosphere, organization, expectations, curricula and teaching practices less likely to trigger the inhibitory effects of down shifting.

Another important insight for educational reform comes from research on brain growth. Epstein reports that the brain grows in alternating periods when growth is rapid and latency periods in which the brain appears to rest. During growth periods the brain is open to 30 large amounts of input and new functioning. During latency periods, the brain seems to concentrate on the consolidation of its experience and is less open to new activities. Epstein points out that schools need to be aware of these periods and adjust the demands made upon students accordingly. He further suggests that overwhelming students with new demands during a latency period may have the effect of turning them off from learning permanently. One of these latency periods falls right at the middle school level and Dr. Epstein suggests that heavy amounts of new demands at that time may be responsible for some of the learning problems that seem to break out in those years.

Psychological Insights

The past thirty to forty years have also seen enormous strides in psychological science and in our understandings about the how and why of human behavior. Such concepts have vast implications for educational theory and practice but to date have had little influence upon the system. Five new areas of psychological exploration, in particular, have important contributions to make to educational reform.

1.A New Frame Of Reference

The goals we seek and the practices we employ in education are direct outcomes of the beliefs we hold about the nature of students and the causes of their behavior. For more than fifty years much of educational theory and practice has been predicated upon the manipulation of forces frame of reference of stimulus- response or behavior modification psychologies. In the early forties a new group of psychologies, called perceptual, or experiential, began to emerge as a new frame of reference from which to understand human behavior and has now come into prominence. According to this view, behavior is regarded as symptom of what is going on inside the behaver. People behave according to how things seem to them. The causes of behavior, accordingly, lie in people's meanings, generally known as perceptions, beliefs, feelings or attitudes about self and the world.

This idea that behavior is a function of personal meaning is consistent with recent findings that the brain is a specialized organ for the processing of meaning. The principle seems self evident. We can check it against our own behavior. We do, indeed, behave according to how things seem to us at the moment of action. So does everyone else. The principle also explains why the manipulation of forces approach to changing behavior is only partly successful. People don't behave directly in response to the forces exerted upon them. They behave according to how things seem to them at the moment of acting. They do not respond directly to the stimulus. They respond to the _personal meaning_ of the stimulus. How teachers respond to a proposed curriculum change, for example, will vary greatly depending upon whether they see the proposal as: a request or a demand, reasonable or another "damned interference", something they know how to do, good or bad for kids, consistent or opposed to their personal philosophy, challenging or threatening, approved by other teachers, too much trouble, too time consuming, or any of a hundred other possibilities. No wonder the manipulation of forces approach so frequently falls short or misfires.

The apparently simple shift in understanding the causes of behavior involved in the perceptual-experiential view has enormous consequences for all sorts of human activities. It is especially significant for educational practice and our attempts at educational reform. For example, it vitally affects our conception of motivation and learning. If behavior is a function of personal meaning, it is not enough simply to manipulate the forces acting on people. Some change must occur in people's beliefs, feeling, attitudes, hopes and aspirations. Furthermore, since the causes of behavior lie inside people, they cannot be directly manipulated. They can only be more or less influenced or facilitated. This changes the necessary role of the teacher from controller, director, instructor to helper, aid or facilitator. Likewise, it calls for administrators who are not so much managers, directors, executives or bosses as consultants, facilitators, providers of means and encouragement. This shift in our basic frame of reference calls for important changes throughout education from nursery school to graduate school. It is also vital for educational reform as we will observe repeatedly throughout this volume.

2.The Importance Of The Self Concept

Among perceptual/experiential psychology's prime contributions, perhaps none is more important than the light it sheds on the nature and functions of the self concept. Modern psychology tells us that every behavior is a direct outcome of how one sees one's self and how one sees the world at the moment of acting. While perceptions of the world may vary greatly from moment to moment, how we see ourselves is much more constant and is involved in everything we do. The self concept is an organization of all the ways we regard ourselves. It is who we refer to when we say, "I" or "me". Each of us has thousands of ways in which we define ourselves, "I am Joe Smith, father, citizen, Democrat, owner of a house on second avenue, divorced, auto mechanic, tennis player," etc., etc.,etc. These self definitions also include value judgements as, "I am a good citizen, poor tennis player, first rate mechanic, tall, short, fat, thin, like pistachio ice cream, the Denver Broncos, hate bigots etc". Whatever the self concept, it affects every behavior, including how students learn, behave or misbehave in school. That goes for teachers and administrators as well. How educators see themselves has a crucial bearing upon the ways they relate to educational reforms.

3.Motivation And Learning

Perceptual/experiential approaches to psychology see motivation and learning quite differently from traditional approaches. The manipulation of forces notion sees motivation as what we do to get others to behave as we desire. The experiential view, confirmed by what we know about the brain, tells us that people are always motivated; they are never unmotivated. People are constantly searching for personal meaning, to make sense of their experience. That is what learning is all about. Learning is the discovery of personal meaning. It happens inside people and cannot be accomplished without the active involvement of the person. These new conceptions of motivation and learning call for important changes in teaching goals and techniques. They are equally significant for planning and acting to change the thinking and practices of educators. These new conceptions are so important for education that we have devoted the entire next chapter to them.

4. Understanding Group Processes

A fourth valuable source of new understanding lies in the area of group dynamics. Workers in psychotherapy, social work, counseling and education have now compiled an extensive literature inquiring into all aspects of group process, philosophy, organization, methodologies, outcomes and the psychology of group leaders. Since most of education is carried on in group settings, these new insights provide a rich source of data for thinking and acting in classrooms, and teacher-pupil relationships. They have equally important contributions to make to the problems of educational reform and the relationships of teachers, supervisors and administrators.

The fields of psychotherapy, social work and counseling are deeply involved in group process. They, too, are concerned with helping clients learn more about themselves and their worlds and to discover more effective and efficient ways of relating to society. They are deeply involved with many of the same goals as education. Insights gained from these disciplines ought to have much significance for education in general and reform in particular. To speed reform, insights from these areas should be utilized as promising guidelines for planning and innovating wherever relevant throughout education.

5. Self Actualization And Health

A fifth source of new understandings of special interest for reform lies in new insights about what it means to be supremely healthy. For many years we have lived with a view of mental health and human adjustment tied to the normal curve. According to this view, well adjusted people are those in the middle with the misfits at either end of the curve. This has never been a very satisfactory picture of mental health. After all, who really wants to be average? About thirty five years ago, many workers began to look at the question in a more promising way. "What", they asked, "Does it mean to be supremely healthy in the highest sense of that term?" "What would a truly self actualized human being be like?" These studies have great importance for education. Whatever we decide is the nature of personal health and human fulfillment must automatically become a major goal for education. Producing healthy, fulfilled human beings is what the system is all about.

These new conceptions have already had considerable impact in the profession. In 1962 the Association For Supervision and Curriculum Development published a yearbook, Perceiving, Behaving, Becoming: A New Focus for Education. In this volume, they reviewed the best thinking available on the notion of self actualization and health. After that, they turned this information over to a nationwide committee of educators from all levels of the system to explore the implications for educational thinking and practice. The book has had an extraordinary effect upon teachers and administrators in many parts of the country and continues to be a best selling yearbook nearing thirty years later. The concepts of this publication and the thinking and research it has spawned since its appearance point the way to exciting innovations for all aspects of the educative process, including efforts at reform.

Summary

In Chapter One we examined some of the current factors making educational reform so pressing an issue for our time. In this chapter we have reviewed the traditional goals of education. To those objectives we have added demands being made by the future into which our youth are moving. We have closed with a brief listing of developments from biology and psychology which shed new light upon the nature of the human organism and how it learns and behaves. Educational practice has fallen far behind the advances made possible by the basic sciences on which it rests. It is not enough simply to adapt to these new principles. We must make certain that our schools will never again fall so far behind the advance of science. We need to build into the system a dynamic quality of self renewal that will assure continuous adaptations in the years ahead.

A crucial problem for any reform movement must be to close the gap between the best we know scientifically and the implications of that knowledge for educational thinking and practice. The remainder of this volume is intended to contribute to that end. Whatever we do in education must be based upon the very best, most up to date thinking we can find about the problems of motivation and learning. In the next chapter, therefore, we begin with an exploration of new knowledge about learning and change with vast implications, not only for the classroom but for the processes of reform as well.

Notes and References On the current scene:

Green, J. 1987. The next wave: A synopsis of recent education reform reports Education Commission of the States, Denver.

Hodgkinson, H. 1985. All one system: Demographics of education, kindergarten through graduate school. Institute for Educational Leadership, Washington, D.C.

Smith, R. and Lincoln, C. 1988. America's shame, America's hope: Twelve million youth at risk. MDC Inc. Chapel Hill,N.C.

Education and the future:

Benjamin, S. 1989. "An ideascope for education: What futurists recommend". Phi Delta Kappan 47,7-13.

Carnegie Corporation, 1986. Carnegie forum on education and the economy, a nation prepared: Teachers for the 21st century. Carnegie Corporation, New York.

Combs, A. 1988. "New assumptions for educational reform" Educational Leadership, 45,38-42.

Combs, A. 1981. "What the future requires of education". Phi Delta Kappan, 62,369-372.

Godet, M. 1988. "Worldwide challenges and crises in education systems.". Futures, 1988, 241-251.

Goodlad, J. 1983. A place called school: prospects for the future. New York, McGraw Hill.

Lewis, J. 1987. Recreating our schools for the 21st century Westbury, N.Y., Wilkerson Publishing.

McCune, S. 1986. Guide to strategy planning for educators. Alexandria, Va. Association for Supervision and Curriculum Development.

Rubin, L. 1975. The future of education: Perspectives on tomorrow's schooling Boston, Allyn and Bacon.

Shane, H. and Tobler, M. 1988. Educating for a new millenium Bloomington, Indiana, Phi Delta Kappa.

32

Toffler, A. 1974. Learning for tomorrow: The role of the future in education, New York, Random House.

The need for self renewing schools:

Goodlad, J. 1987. The ecology of school renewal. Chicago, University of Chicago Press.

Gordon, D. 1984. The myths of school self renewal New York, Teacher's College Press.

Shane, H. 1989. "Educated foresight for the 90's". Educational Leadership 47,4-6.
36

The need for new curricula:

Apple, M. 1989. "Curriculum in the year 2000: Tensions and possibilities". Phi Delta Kappan, 64,321-326.

Berman, L. and Roderick, J. 1987. "Future curricular priorities". Education Research Quarterly 1,4, 79-87.

Glines, D. 1978. "What competencies will be needed in the future". Thrust for Educational Leadership, 7, 4,24- 28.

Howard, E. 1989. "A futures oriented change model". IN Hennes, J. Restructuring education: Strategic options required for excellence. Denver, Co. Colorado Department of Education.

Van Avery, D. 1979. Futuristics and education: An ASCD task force report. Alexandria, Va., Association for Supervision and Curriculum Development.

Van Avery, D. 1980. "Futuristics and education". Educational Leadership 37, 441-442.

On lifelong learning:

Cetron, M. 1988. "Class of 2000: The good news and the bad news." The Futurist, 1988,9-15.

Combs, A. 1981. "What the future demands of education"Phi Delta Kappan, 62, 269-372.

Goodlad, J. et. al. 1987. The ecology of school renewal: NSSE yearbook, Part 1., Chicago, University of Chicago Press.

On responsible citizenship and global schools:

Anderson,B and Cox,P. 1988. Configuring the educational system for a shared future. Denver, Co. Educational Commission of the states.

Becker, J. 1979. Schooling for a global age. New York. McGraw Hill.

Boyer, E. 1988 "The future of American education: New realities, making connections" Kappa Delta Phi Record
6-12.

Etzioni,A. 1982. "Education for mutuality and civility". The Futurist, 16, 4-7.

Kniep, W. 1990 "Global education as school reform". Educational Leadership 47,43-46.

Larsh,E. 1989. "Getting the herd headed west: rationale and processes". IN Hennes, J. Restructuring education: Strategic options required for excellence Denver, Co. Colorado Department of Education.

Wilson, T. 1985. "The global environment and the quest for peace: A revolution in the scale of things". Social Education, 49,201-204.

On brain research:

Epstein, H. 1974. "Phenoblysis:special brain and mind growth periods. I Human brain and skull development." Developmental Psychobiology 7,302-216.

Epstein, H. 1974. "Phenoblysis: special brain and mind growth periods. II Human mental development." Developmental Psychobiology, 7,217-224.

Hart, L. 1983. Human brain and human learning New York, Longman.

Hart, L. 1989. "The horse is dead". Phi Delta Kappan, 71,237-242.

On perceptual-experiential psychology:

Combs, A. and Avila, D. Helping relationships: Basic concept for the helping professions Boston,Ma. Allyn and Bacon.

34

Combs, A., Richards, A. and Richards,F. Perceptual Psychology: A humanistic approach to the study of persons Lanham, Md. ,University Press of America.

On group process in education:

Hunter, E. 1972. Encounter in the classroom. New York, Holt, Rinehart.

Kemp,C. 1970 Perspectives on the group process. Boston, Houghton-Mifflin.

Schmuck, P. 1971. Group process in the classroom. Dubuque, Iowa, Wm. Brown.

On new understanding about learning:

American Federation of Teachers. 1986. The revolution that is overdue: Looking toward the future of teaching and learning. Eric Clearing House in Teacher Education.

Combs, A. See titles above.

Heckman, P. 1987. "Understanding school cultures" IN Goodlad, J. The ecology of school renewal. Chicago, University of Chicago Press.

On new conceptions of health.

ASCD 1962. Perceiving, behaving, becoming: A new focus for education. Alexandria, Va. Yearbook of the Association for Supervision and Curriculum Development.

Combs, A.W. 1981. "Humanistic education: Too tender for a tough world?". Phi Delta Kappan, 62, 446-449.

Jourard, S. and Landsman, T. 1980. Healthy personality: An approach from humanistic psychology. New York. Macmillan.

Chapter 3

Motivation And Learning

Whatever is done to construct an effective system of education must be predicated upon the very best information available about the nature of learning and motivation. A major reason why current schools need restructuring is that former conceptions of how people learn and why they engage in the process have drastically changed in the past thirty years. Schools and teaching formulated under the old assumptions are no longer adequate for today's youth and modern goals of education. It seems elementary that whatever we attempt in reforming our schools should be based upon the best, most adequate conceptions of learning available. Instead, the question is rarely raised by reformers who blithely advocate one change or another without reference to its effect upon the learning process. The result; strategies which are palliative at best, which create more problems than they solve, or at worst, may be downright destructive.

Motivation And Learning: The Foundation For Reform

Most of our current approaches to teaching are based upon ideas about motivation and learning now recognized by many psychologists to be only partially relevant, outmoded by current research and practice. Until recently, we have understood behavior as the consequence of forces exerted on the individual. In that frame of reference, motivation becomes a matter of manipulating the forces exerted on the student to get him/her to do what the teacher wishes. From that same way of thinking, learning is change in behavior generally brought about through such external forces as: reward, punishment or the experience of positive or negative consequences. Beginning from such an assumption learning is fostered in the classroom through reliance upon lecture, demonstration, modeling, telling, recitation and reinforced by various forms of approbation, grades, praise, criticism, reward or punishment. The same manipulation of forces philosophy is applied in the processes of school management and efforts at school reform.

Since the facilitation of learning is the primary purpose of education, whatever strategies for reform we devise must begin from the best we know about the learning process. What modern science has to tell us about the principles of learning are the basic assumptions from which we must start at whatever level we choose to intervene in the system. Whether we are concerned about student growth, curricula, teacher-student relationships, programs, schools, administration or national planning the principles of learning must play a major role in thought and action. Basic principles of learning cannot be ignored because they are inconvenient. Ignoring what we know about learning is like saying, "I know my car needs a carburetor but I'm going to drive mine without one."

In the past thirty years we have acquired a new and more adequate conception of motivation and learning with ramifications for every aspect of education; for the classroom, administration, supervision, professional training and the processes of reform as well. In this chapter we will consider seven basic principles from this new thinking of special importance for educational reform. We begin with the question of motivation.

1. Motivation

The Traditional View

From the customary manipulation of forces viewpoint, motivation is what the leader does to get people to behave the way he/she desires. The strategy is familiar to everyone. One sets up a system of rewards for conformity with the new requirement and/or provides appropriate punishments for non-compliance. The strategy may be further refined by carefully eliminating the possibility of undesirable choices. The overall plan is familiar to anyone who has ever lived in the country and set out to bring the cows in from pasture. Proceeding from the barn to the pasture one opens gates where the cows should go and closes those where they must not. One then calls the cows to the barn (reward) or gets behind the herd to shout or wield a switch to urge them forward (punishment). A fencing in strategy works fine with cows and they generally make their way up the prepared pathway to their stanchions in the barn. The plan works much less well with people. People have a maddening way of finding gates we forgot to close or climbing over the fences to scatter over the countryside.

Actually, the manipulation of forces approach is not motivation: it is management. As we have seen in Chapter One, the trouble with the manipulation of forces approach is not that it is wrong, but that it is only partly right. People do, indeed, sometimes respond to the manipulation of forces in hoped for ways. Unfortunately, they do not do so often enough to make the strategy trustworthy or efficient. We need a more accurate view of what motivates people from which to attack the problems of improving education.

Need And Motivation

Of all the things that psychologists know about change in human behavior, of this we are most certain--- that people learn best when they have a need to know. True motivation happens inside people. It has to do with people's wants, needs, desires, wishes and goals. Modern experiential psychology tells us that all behavior is determined by the fundamental need of the organism. From birth to death each of us is engaged in a continuous search for personal fulfillment. That drive provides the fundamental basis for motivation.

The maintenance and enhancement of our selves, including the persons or things with whom we identify, is the motive power behind all behavior. This force exists in every cell of our being. It is so important that the profession of medicine depends upon it. Doctors do not cure us. They minister to our basic need by prescribing rest, diet or medicines to kill or inhibit invading organisms, or they may operate to repair an afflicted organ. In the final analysis, it is the body itself which recovers. This universal search of the organism provides the driving force for every behavior. True motivation has to do with what people feel they need to do or think to maintain or enhance their selves. In this sense, people are always motivated; they are never unmotivated. They may not be interested in doing what you or I wish for them, but they are always motivated to seek fulfillment of their personal needs.

Personal need takes precedence over all others. The child with a deep need to be accepted by his friend finds it necessary to communicate with her in spite of the teacher's admonitions to "mind your own business" or "work alone". Similarly, the harried teacher, concerned with a personal need about "getting through this day" is unlikely to welcome additional demands imposed by some well meant reform. The need to maintain and enhance the self is so fundamental to the organism's existence that it can rarely be set aside, except for very short periods. When confronted with a variety of demands, it is only those which seem most personally satisfying and immediate that are likely to motivate behavior.

Real And Artificial Needs

When assigned tasks are at odds with personal needs, you can count on it, students, teachers or administrators will find ingenious ways to fulfill their own needs first. They do this, not because they are lazy, hostile or intent upon sabotage. They do it because they are human. That is how everyone behaves. It is in "the nature of the beast" to seek fulfillment of personal needs. When the demands of others are consistent with those needs, we go along willingly. When they are not, we ignore the demand, pretend to carry it out or distort it in some fashion to make it fit our own needs.

It is a human quality to believe that what seems good to me will seem equally good to other intelligent human beings. As a consequence, reformers, enamored of the innovation they hope to introduce, assume that teachers will see it as desirable too. Or, "By George, if they don't ,they should!" Getting people to see the necessity for action or information is a universal problem for education. It is a constant puzzler for every classroom teacher. It is equally frustrating for the processes of reform. To be effective, demands made upon people must be seen as personally relevant. Ignoring the personal needs of the critical actors whether they be students, teachers or administrators can doom even the most promising proposals to ignominious defeat.

One way teachers have sought to deal with this dilemma is to create artificial needs for knowing or behaving. So, schools have used grades and grading, reward and punishment systems, prizes, competitions or a thousand devices to provide students with external inducements for acceding to educational plans. In similar fashion, administrators, supervisors, school boards, and state legislatures have resorted to artificial devices for motivation to reform. Among these are salary increases or bonuses, paid vacations, travel privileges, summer tuition, teacher of the year awards, reprimands, supervisory visits and many more. Mostly these prove to be disappointing. Worse still, they are frequently accompanied by side effects which complicate or subvert the change process. When the chips are down, it is only personal needs that can be counted upon for sustained and creative action.

Remote and Immediate Needs

Immediate needs always seem more pressing than remote ones so have greater motivating potential. The promise of Christmas has little motivating force for a child in July. The closer the event comes to realization, the more children become excited, building up to breathless anticipation on Christmas Eve. Similarly, a teacher's immediate need to deal with an obstreperous child takes precedence over professional goals; even over personal resolutions. The force of immediate needs versus remote ones is equally relevant for educational reform. Educators at every level are much more strongly motivated by immediate needs than those farther off.

It is widely assumed that models are important motivators for youth. So, outstanding men and women are constantly held up as examples to be emulated. In fact, their motivational value has been grossly exaggerated. The effect of models is subject to the same immediate or remote principles noted above. People are far more likely to be motivated by friends or acquaintances who are contacted daily than persons of sterling qualities far removed from personal experience. Generally speaking, the greater the gap between a model and ourselves, the weaker the motivating force. For nearly two thousand years we have extolled the perfection of Christ but most of us still fall far short of His example.

Despite the importance of need for the learning process, few schools give more than lip service to the notion. Information and the curriculum is delivered to students willy nilly whether they see any need for it or not. Likewise, rules are made, grading systems are established, schedules and hours are set and teaching methods are chosen more often to fill the needs of teachers and administrators than to advance the learning process. Too often students are expected or coerced to comply with rules, regulations, practices or curricular decisions they had no voice in establishing. It is human nature to seek out what we need and to escape from groups and events that are not personally fulfilling. Current failure to meet the needs of youth is clearly observable in the drop out rate, discipline problems and shocking achievement records. The common cry of students that "school is so irrelevant" is merely another way of saying, "schools don't meet our needs". An up dated, restructured school system must find more adequate ways to recognize the importance of personal need for learning and must adapt its schools and teaching accordingly.

Reactions To Demands For Change.

Demands for change may be quickly accepted and put into practice when they promise satisfaction of personal need. Demands contrary to personal needs are almost never successful. Instead, they may be ignored in whole or in part. Teachers who are asked or ordered to operate in unfamiliar or objectionable ways may simply ignore the new regulations altogether. After all, when the classroom door is closed, nobody know what goes on in there but the teacher and the students. Most of the time the students are not sure either. If the strategy of total disregard is not possible, there are dozens of ways to give the impression of compliance while actually subverting the intent. Ingenious teachers or administrators have even been known to find ways to manipulate the requirements of bosses for the advancement of their own purposes.

Two Options For Teaching Or Reform

The crucial relationship of personal need to motivation leaves teachers and reformers with two options;

1. they can relate learning or innovations to the existing personal needs of those who are engaged in the process.

or, 2. they must, somehow, <u>create</u> appropriate personal needs in the belief systems of the critical persons.

The first of these options is by far the most effective. Needs created by outsiders rarely have the urgency of personal needs and so run the risk of being treated as irrelevant. It has been said that the genius of good teaching lies not merely in fulfilling student needs but in helping students discover needs they never knew they had. The principle is equally true for the processes of reform. We need to relate desired changes to the existing needs of teachers or find ways to create new ones.

2. The Effects Of Challenge And Threat

A second vital observation about motivation has to do with the effects of challenge and threat. People feel challenged when they are confronted with problems that interest them and which they feel reasonably able to solve. People feel threatened when they are confronted with problems they do not feel able to handle.

The Nature Of Challenge

People are challenged by matters that seem to them likely to satisfy their basic need for maintenance and enhancement of self. When that assessment is combined with the feeling of being able to achieve it, the potential for motivation is very great. Under such conditions people will expend enormous amounts of time and energy to achieve their goals. They will even suffer pain or humiliation to achieve objectives if the challenge seems great enough. Witness: The child learning to ride a bike who takes tumble after tumble but gets up to try again. Or, the investor who takes a chance in the stock market. Or, the woman who tries out for a part in a play despite the possible embarrassment of stagefright.

The Experience Of Threat

When people feel threatened they are also motivated to act but in far less positive fashion. The experience of threat has two unhappy effects upon behavior. Psychologists call one of these, "tunnel vision". Under threat a person's field of perceptions becomes narrowed down to the object of threat, much like looking at things through a tunnel. The experience is familiar to anyone who has ever experienced worry or a dangerous situation. The worry keeps intruding on other observations as one's mind reverts time and again to the worrisome matter. Or, after a near miss while driving, one may find herself saying, "the only thing I could see was that big truck coming at me!". When asked by her father, "What did you learn today?", a child replied,

"Nuthin! But was my teacher mad! Wow!" In the face of an angry teacher the only thing that held her attention was her teacher's anger. Under threat the ability to perceive becomes narrowed to the threatening object or event. Tunnel vision had survival value in the course of evolution assuring the organism's attention to dangerous objects or events. It seriously interferes with the learning process. The tunnel vision response to threat is clearly the reverse of what is needed for effective learning or educational reform.

The second effect of threat forces a person to defend her existing position. Since the basic need of the organism is for maintenance and enhancement, any threat to self demands attention and mobilization for defense. Accordingly, threatened persons are motivated to defend themselves at all costs. The hotter the argument gets the more people tend to stick to the position they held in the first place. Any parent or teacher who has ever tried to get a frightened child who has misbehaved to change his story knows this reaction well. It happens in grown ups too. Who has not experienced the frustration of dealing with someone "who just can't see how wrong he is!" Likewise, the self defensive reaction to threat is antithetic to effective reform. We need folks ready and willing to see more broadly and experiment with better ways of operating.

These two effects of threat, self defense and tunnel vision, explain why it is that people can only be taught what not to do by threats. Threat is rarely helpful in the production of positive change. Effective education must find ways to challenge students without threatening them. The effects of challenge and threat also have important bearings upon the problems of reform. To motivate people toward needed reform, it will be necessary to find ways of eliminating or ameliorating the experience of threat. Both effects of threat are disruptive. We need to open and broaden the perceptions of teachers and administrators, not narrow them. Likewise, we need to facilitate change, not force the defense of established ways of doing things. Effective reform requires challenging teachers and administrators with problems that interest them and which seem to them to lie within their capacities to resolve.

A common complaint about the profession is that teachers, administrators or students "are so apathetic!". They just don't seem to get excited about the need for learning or innovation. It does little good to berate people for being apathetic. Apathy is not a cause. It is a result, a normal response to lack of challenge.

The implications of challenge and threat for reform are crystal clear. Somehow we must find better ways of challenging students without threatening them. At the classroom level that calls for widespread changes in all sorts of areas: curriculum content and requirements, teacher-student relationships, methods and strategies of teaching as well as school rules, regulations and organization. Applied to school personnel, the processes of reform must seem to those who must carry them out to be self fulfilling enough for active engagement and charged with a minimum of personal risk.

3. The Personal Character Of Learning And Change

Change In Belief--The Function Of Education

According to modern perceptual-experiential psychology, the basic principle of learning can be stated as follows: <u>Any information will affect a person's behavior only in the degree to which the person has discovered the personal meaning of the information to his/her self</u>. To illustrate: Riding in my car on the way to work, I turn on the radio and hear the latest hog market quotations. (Position A, Figure 1) Not having any hogs this

Figure 4 - 1
Learning And Personal Meaning

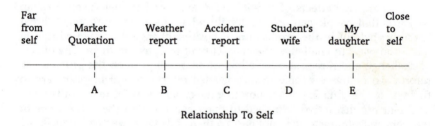

Relationship To Self

information has no relevance for me. "It goes in one ear and out the other", as the saying goes. Next, I hear the weather report (Position B) which has a little more bearing upon my personal needs and I am pleased that it is going to be a nice day. The news report which follows (Position C) lets me know that there has been a serious accident near the University and Ms. Nancy Collins has been seriously injured and taken to the hospital. I do not know Ms. Collins, but I am a person driving a car near the University, so this information has more personal meaning to me. It also affects my behavior more. I say to myself, "Another accident. That's terrible" and I slow down for a block or two. Suppose now, that Ms. Collins is the wife of one of my students (Position D.) Now the information has more relevance and produces more response. I think about it for the rest of my drive. When I reach the office, I ask if others have heard about it. I mention it to my colleagues and inquire how Bill Collins is fixed financially. Now imagine what happens to my behavior if Nancy Collins is the married name of my daughter! (Position E) The closer the relationship of information to the self, the greater is the degree of action it produces.

Learning is the discovery of personal meaning. It always has two parts: one, confrontation with some event or information and the other, the discovery of its personal meaning. Traditional education does very well with the first half of that equation. We are experts at giving people information. Where we have not done so well is with the second part, helping students discover the personal meaning of the information provided. The drop out, for example, is not a drop out because he wasn't told. He dropped out because he never perceived the personal meaning of what he was told. People do not behave according to the facts or information. They act in terms of what things mean to them--what they think, feel or believe.

Discovering Personal Meaning

It is widely assumed that people aren't learning anything unless they are exposed to new information. This is a serious error. Provision of new information or experience may often be quite unnecessary for effective learning. Some of our most important learnings, for example, have nothing to do with new information. Few of us need more information, for example, about the idea of the "brotherhood of man". What is needed is a deeper and deeper discovery of the meaning of that idea in our personal belief systems. Research studies on good and poor teachers show that both groups are knowledgeable about education and teaching but, clearly, only the good ones operate on their knowledge. Teachers and administrators already have all the information they need for many a reform effort. What is required to put that information into practice is only a broader, deeper perception of its personal meaning for those who must put it to work in the classroom.

Learning Takes Time

Giving information is quick and easy; facilitating the discovery of meaning takes time and commitment to the process. Failure to understand this fact is a major reason why many reform attempts come to nothing. People do not change quickly. How quickly a person can change will depend, in part, on the discrepancy between his/her existing position and the hoped for reform. The greater the discrepancy, the more time and effort will be required to bring it about.

Understanding learning as the discovery of personal meaning changes the most basic assumption upon which education must be founded. It swings the focus of education from teaching, the delivery of information or skill, to learning, what is going on inside the learner. Learning, in this view is a complex, deeply personal and individual experience. To nurture it properly requires valuing and understanding the learner and the construction of learning environments and strategies accordingly. It underscores the need for individualizing instruction that we have so often touted but seldom committed ourselves to accomplish. Furthermore, since change in personal meaning happens inside students and is not directly open to manipulation, the role of the teacher must shift from controller, director, teacher, to helper, aid, facilitator and friendly representative of society. A personal meaning conception of learning calls for person-centered schools and teachers in place of the subject matter concentration typical of the majority of our current schools and faculties.

4. The Self Concept And Learning

In addition to its involvement in the process of discovering meaning, the self concept has another important effect upon learning and change. Among the scientific advances briefly mentioned in the previous chapter, is the crucial character of the self concept in human behavior. The beliefs people have about themselves affect everything they do---including their responses to learning and change. People behave according to how things seem to them, especially how they see themselves and the worlds they must confront. That fact, in itself, should be enough to make the developing self concepts of students a major concern for education and reform. Even more important for education, we know that what students believe about themselves has vital effects upon their abilities to learn. Most children brought to reading clinics, for example, believe they can't read. Because they believe that, they do not try. Because they do not try, they get no practice. Because they get no practice, they don't learn. Then, when the teacher asks them to read, they read badly, causing the teacher to remark, "My goodness! You don't read very well". Getting the parents into the act by sending home a low report card grade only confirms the idea and corroborates what the child believed in the first place!

Self concepts are of even greater importance because of their self corroborative character. The child or adult who believes he can't do math, speak before an audience, play tennis or whatever, avoids the experience so does not improve. Then, when he/she must perform, the weak performance only serves to prove what the person felt in the beginning. A major tragedy of our society is the existence of millions of people who believe they can do only X much. Accordingly, that is all the much they do. Others, observing this behavior conclude, "Well, that's just an X much person". So, the behavior is perpetuated and the person continues to operate far below his/her capacity. Our schools ought not contribute to this shameful waste of human potential.

Supremely healthy persons, we are told, see themselves in essentially positive ways. They see themselves as liked, wanted, acceptable, able, persons of dignity and integrity. As a consequence they make enormous contributions to our society. Unhealthy, maladjusted persons, on the other hand, see themselves as unliked, unwanted, etc. It is not the students who see themselves as liked and wanted who cause teachers difficulty. It is the ones who feel they are unliked, unwanted, unable who are the misfits and problems as children and who grow up to fill our jails and mental hospitals. Whether people are likely to be successful, happy and self fulfilled is largely dependent upon the nature of their self concepts. The principle applies to teachers and administrators too. Research has demonstrated that good teachers see themselves in essentially positive ways while poor ones see themselves in negative fashion. So, an important goal of educational reform must be to select school personnel with positive self concepts or assist teachers and administrators to develop them on the job.

People are not born with their self concepts. They learn them from the ways they have been treated in the course of growing up. Beliefs about self are learned, especially from interactions with the significant people in our lives. Being a significant other in the lives of students is exactly what schools and teachers are supposed to be. Education cannot escape affecting student self concepts. It can only choose to provide positive or negative experiences or leave the matter to chance. In light of all available evidence we can only conclude that a major objective of education must be the fostering of positive self concepts in its students.

Little by little the importance of student self concepts for healthy learning and growth is beginning to affect the thinking and practices of our public schools but the process is far too slow given the importance of the issue. Most current schools operate with little thought to student self concepts. Few of today's teachers are totally ignorant of the self concept and its effects but even those who know about it have not yet incorporated the idea sufficiently into personal meaning to affect their teaching behavior. Implementation of this important principle requires more than lip service and half hearted application. The crucial character of the self concept in behavior requires person-centered schools and teachers keenly aware of the dynamics of self concept for student growth and development and systematically applying that knowledge to every aspect of planning and practice.

5. Feeling And Personal Meaning

Effective learning and change is an emotional as well as a personal experience. Generally speaking, the greater the personal meaning of an idea or event, the greater the feeling one has about it. In the listening to the car radio example, illustrated in Figure 1, as meaning becomes more personal emotion increases. (Refer to Figure 2.) There is little or no feeling about hog market quotations, some feeling occurs with the weather report. Hearing about an accident produces somewhat more. Recognition that the injured person is related to one's student, causes the amount of feeling to rise sharply. It becomes extreme with the realization that it is one's daughter who has been injured.

This relationship between personal meaning and emotion has important implications for education and change. Learning is the discovery of personal meaning. The strength of feeling is indicative of the degree of personal meaning. If that is so, then we must have affective education or run the risk of having none at all! The idea that important learnings can be brought about by purely intellectual measures, the weight of evidence, objectivity or facts is a fallacy. People do not behave according to the facts. They behave according to their personal feelings and beliefs. Too many

Figure 4 - 2
Emotion And Learning

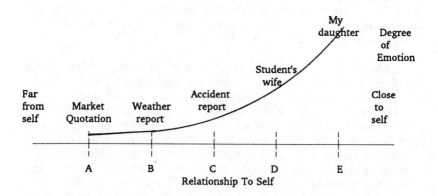

traditional schools seek to operate in the "no nonsense", purely objective fashion of the seventeen or eighteen hundreds when schools were grim and joyless places and teaching proceeded to "the tune of the hickory stick". If learning is, indeed, the deeply human, personal experience that modern psychology assures us it is, then the schools we seek must also be warm, human places. A school system which inculcates fear or loathing for learning has failed both the student and society.

Similarly, there is unlikely to be any effective change in teachers without a degree of feeling. If the persons expected to carry out a needed reform have no feeling about it, nothing much is likely to happen. Simply knowing about a technique or idea is not enough. Participants must be personally committed. Projected reforms must have some personal meaning. Sole reliance upon intellectual approaches for reform is almost certain to result in lack of commitment and disappointing results. Even scientists, who are generally assumed to be models of objectivity are nothing of the sort. They fight tooth and claw for the things they believe in. Several researches on good and poor helpers, including teachers, administrators, counselors and public office holders, demonstrate that objectivity and things orientation is characteristic of poor performers. Effective practitioners focus on subjective, people oriented concerns.

6. Learning And Change Is A Social Function

It is a common assumption among many teachers and educators that learning is best achieved when people work alone. Accordingly, children may be reprimanded for helping their friends or for studying together. Cooperation is called cheating and is widely regarded as reprehensible. As a matter of fact effective learning is far more likely to occur when people are working in congenial groups. To get some notion of the importance of relationships for the learning process, one need but ask him/her self, "What words do I use to describe how I feel when I know I am wanted and belong?" Most people will respond with such terms as, "I feel good, interested, excited, I want to be involved" and the like. If we now ask what words are used to describe personal feelings when one is alienated or outside the group, such terms as these come to mind; depressed, humiliated, embarrassed, left out, "I want to get away from there". Or, if the feeling of alienation is very strong, there may be desires to strike back. Examining these two lists, it is clear which set of attitudes is more likely to result in effective learning or change.

Classrooms organized in rigid rows wherein communication among students is frowned upon create their own impediments to effective learning. Human beings are naturally social. Preventing human relationships flies in the face of what we know about students and how they best learn. How much better to work with the organism through person-centered schools and procedures than against the students' natural tendencies.

The need for group approaches to learning and change in the classroom applies as well to the problem of reform. It is a strange paradox that teaching, a quintessential human activity, is an extraordinarily isolated profession. One would think that after spending long hours with children daily, that teachers would seek relationships with other adults, especially those with problems similar to their own. In fact, teachers in most schools rarely communicate with each other about professional matters. Conversations in the teachers lounge seldom reach beyond the mundane. Most teachers are afraid of each other and doubtful that their classroom activities will bear up under scrutiny. This lack of professional pride and resistance to communicating with each other is a major roadblock to reform. It seems clear that any comprehensive plan must find ways to reaffirm the significance of the teaching profession on one hand and to facilitate communication within the profession on the other.

7. Feedback In Learning And Change

Whenever people undertake to change what they think or do, they need useable feedback about their efforts. Here are four criteria which vitally affect the feedback process:

1. Feedback should be immediate. The value and usefulness of feedback rapidly decreases with the passage of time. Every effort should be expended to provide it at the earliest possible moment after the event to which it relates.

2. Feedback should be personal rather than comparative. It is commonly assumed that comparison with others is a valuable device for motivating people and helping them learn. The notion is only partly true. Much more helpful for effective learning and change is personal feedback; information immediately relevant to one's own performance. Information about what I am doing and what I need to do next is far more useful than being told that I am better than Joe but worse than Mary. Such information is a judgement about me and a digression from the task at hand.

3. Feedback should be directly related to the event. Extraneous feedback turns the person's attention from the task at hand to focus on unrelated events. For many years I praised my students with comments like, "Hey, I like that!", "That's good", "You did a good job" or "I think that's great!" Then, a wise teacher pointed out to me that comments like that put the locus of satisfaction in the wrong place---on pleasing me. To keep the satisfaction in the task or accomplishment I now try to say things like, "Look at that! Last week you couldn't do that", "I'll bet it feels good to know that you can do that" or, "Now that you can do it, will you please go help Sandy

who is having trouble with that problem." Applied to reform, the personal satisfaction of the innovation should be inherent in the reform process itself.

4. Effective feedback should point the way to next steps. Feedback which helps the performer to assess where he is and see where she needs to go next is most likely to be helpful whether in the classroom or in faculty efforts at reform.

Applying these criteria to traditional grading practices, it becomes clear that grades and grading fail on every count. They are not immediate. They are comparative rather than personal. They are extraneous to the performance and they certainly do not point the way to next steps.

Many a promising lesson in the classroom or innovation in a school has been killed off or discouraged by lack of helpful feedback to the persons attempting the task. One usually has to be tough skinned to be an innovator for most of the feedback received is of a negative character. "You can't do that", "It will never work", "What will people say?", "You're going to cause trouble for the rest of us", "We already did that" or "It's just a fad. It will pass."

Summary

The principles suggested in this chapter apply throughout the educational process, wherever learning and change are to be sought. They are equally applicable to the classroom, counseling office, pre-service or in-service education, supervision or administration. They apply as well to efforts at innovation and reform. Within the classroom they provide the basic assumptions for teacher planning, relationships with students and for the invention of effective methods of teaching. They also represent the fundamental frame of reference for the formulation of educational strategies and tactics. They point to a need for person-centered classrooms, programs and schools and for person-centered teachers and administrators to bring them into fruition.

Notes and References

General references:

Combs, A. and Avila, D. 1985. Helping relationships: Basic concepts for the helping professions Boston, Allyn and Bacon.

Combs, A.W. 1976. "Affective-humanistic learning." In <u>Learning: An overview and update</u> Report of Chief School Officers 1976 Summer Conference, Washington, D.C. Office of Education..

Elkind, D. 1989. "Developmentally appropriate practice: Philosophical and practical imperatives." <u>Phi Delta Kappan</u>. 71,113-117.

Ferguson, M. 1981. <u>The aquarian conspiracy: Personal and social transformation in the 1980's</u>. Los Angeles, P.J. Tarsher.

Larsh, E. 1989. "Change: The seed and the strategic options" IN Hennes, J. <u>Restructuring Education: Strategic options required for excellence.</u> 15-24. Denver, Co. Colorado Department of Education.

Rogers, C. 1967. "The interpersonal relationship in the facilitation of learning". IN <u>Humanizing Education: The Person in the process</u>, Alexandria, Va. Association for Supervision and Curriculum Development.

On motivation and need.

Combs, A. 1971. "Two views of motivation" IN Frymier, J. <u>Handbook of research on human motivation</u>, Columbus, Oh. Ohio State University Press.

Maslow, A. 1970. <u>Motivation and personality</u>, New York. Harper and Row.

On challenge and threat:

Combs, A. and Taylor, C. 1952. "The effect of the perception of mild degrees of threat upon performance". <u>Journal of Abnormal and Social Psychology</u>. 47,420-424.

Goldberg, M. 1966. <u>The effects of ability grouping</u>. New York, Teachers College Press.

On new concepts about learning:

Combs, A. 1966. "Fostering self direction". <u>Educational Leadership</u> 23,373-387.

Combs, A. 1973. "The human side of learning". <u>The National Elementary Principal</u>, 52, 38-43.

Harvey, O. 1970. "Belief and behavior: Some implications for education." <u>The Science Teacher</u>, 37, 10-14.

On self concept and learning:

Aspy, D. and Roebuck, F. 1976. A lever long enough. Washington, D.C., Consortium for Humanizing Education.

Combs, A. and Soper, D. 1962. "The self, its derivate terms and research". Journal of Individual Psychology. 13,134-145.

Fitts, W. 1971. The self concept and self actualization. Nashville, TN. Dede Wallace Center.

Hamachek,D. 1976. The self in growth, teaching and learning. Englewood Cliffs, N.J., Prentice Hall.

Lamy, M. 1965. "Relationship of self perceptions in early primary children to achievement in reading" Doctoral dissertation, Gainesville, FL. University of Florida.

Purkey, W. 1970. Self concept and school achievement. Englewood Cliffs, N.J., Prentice Hall.

On affective education:

Aspy, D. and Roebuck, F. 1977 Kids don't learn from teachers they don't like. Amherst, Ma. Human Resources Development Press.

Combs, A. 1967. Humanizing education: The persons in the process. Alexandria, Va. Association for Supervision and Curriculum Development.

On social aspects of learning:

Langberg, A. 1989. "Caring and engagement". IN Hennes, J. Restructuring education: Strategic options required for excellence. Denver, Co. Colorado Department of Education.

On feedback and grading:

Kirschenbaum, H. and Simon, S. 1971. Wad ja get? ; The grading game in American education. New York, Hart Publishing.

Shepard, L. and Smith, M. 1989. Flunking grades; Research and policies on retention Philadelphia, Pa. Palmer Press.

Simon, S. and Ballance, J. 1976. <u>Degrading the grading myth: A primer of alternatives to grades and marks</u>. Alexandria, a. Association for Supervision and Curriculum Development.

CHAPTER 4

PERSON-CENTERED SCHOOLS AND TEACHERS

From what is now clear about our changing society and from new understanding about human biology and the learning process, what sorts of schools and teachers do we need? To lift us out of the quagmire we are in and to guard against falling into similar rigidities in the future, we need a self renewing system; one that is continuously sensitive to the changing needs of society and youth on one hand and readily adaptable to the advances of physical and social science on the other.

In the current press for reform innumerable remedies are being proposed. Most of these are specific suggestions for structure, methods or curricula advocated as "oughts" or "shoulds" to be implemented across the boards. Such specificity can only add to current rigidities and postpone achievement of the self renewing system we so desperately require.

The Myth of "Right" Methods

It would seem an easy way to get started setting up person-centered schools on a larger scale would be simply to find out what person-centered teachers are doing around the nation and then to apply their techniques to one's local problems. Unfortunately, the matter is not so simple. One of the assumptions that has brought traditional education to its current unhappy state, is the belief that reforms can be brought about by legislating or ordering their introduction into schools. As a matter of fact, millions of man-hours and hundreds of millions of dollars have been spent trying to find good or right methods for teaching or administering but we are still unable to discriminate any method or technique that is clearly associated with either good or bad practice. Despite this discouraging history, research along such lines continues unabated. The literature abounds with reports from groups and individuals, burning with enthusism for one method or another that has worked for them, offering their special techniques, gadgets or ways of organizing as the new solution for educational reform. Alas, with no greater promise than those that have gone before.

One reason why we cannot find widely applicable good or right methods of teaching is the fact that methods are extremely complex. Even the simplest strategy must fit an enormous number of conditions. Here are just a few. They must fit the local conditions: the room, time, equipment, supplies, temperature, lighting etc. They must fit the subject matter in all its complexity. They must fit the student; especially student needs, individual differences, readiness, rates of progress, capacity, motivation, previous experience, interests and physical condition. They must also fit the teacher, including the teacher's personality, preparation, knowledge, belief systems, feelings, attitudes and characteristic ways of thinking and acting.

Finding a particular method right for such diverse conditions is clearly a hopeless task. Even the best of methods suggested by master teachers, writers, administrators or supervisors must be tailored to fit a particular teacher and whatever students and conditions he/she is currently confronting. Any method may work for some teacher at some place at some time. The methods teachers use are only symptoms of the teacher's highly personal purposes and perceptions. They represent the teacher's attempts to find a way to deal with a complex set of curricula, goals, students and local conditions. Effective teaching is not a mechanical function. It requires professional, creative persons capable of confronting problems and finding appropriate solutions, not only in long time planning but also, from moment to moment in response to changing conditions or opportunities.

Seeking reform through mandated methods or procedures only commits teachers to less important goals. For example, one effect of the press for behavioral objectives in the last decade was to concentrate teacher attention upon specific behaviors that could be quickly achieved and precisely measured. This often had the effect of focusing teacher attention upon simplistic goals so that larger objectives were neglected. Methods mandated by well-meaning legislators, school boards, superintendents or administrators often do little more than increase the frustrations of what is already a demanding task for conscientious teachers. They may even hinder the very objectives they were designed to fulfill. Recent national assessments of achievement in mathematics, for example, suggest that an unexpected outcome of the "back to basics" movement in teaching math is a decrease in student problem solving capacities. Preoccupation with specifics apparently had the effect of causing the neglect of broader, more important objectives. Methods that fence teachers in, inhibit creativity or create debilitating anxieties may prove too big a price to pay.

A second reason why concentration upon methods is inadequate for reform lies in the fact that the effectiveness of methods can only be judged in terms of what the encounter meant to the student. The effect of any method is not a result of the method itself but of its peculiar meaning to the student. Accordingly, methods must be judged by the messages they convey. The message received by a student may be very different from what an outsider might report was happening or even what the teacher intended. Methods can even carry messages capable of destroying intended outcomes or distorting them so as to produce totally unexpected results. Sometimes these are amusing. They may also subvert entire programs or boomerang to destroy the very goals they were intended to achieve.

Methods must be understood as individual matters that teachers must explore and discover for themselves. That should be good news for teachers. Since there are no universal right or good methods, they can be who they are, do their own thing, teach in their own peculiar ways and still be good teachers. It also means that teachers cannot be judged fairly on the basis of the methods they use. Nor can certain methods be demanded of teachers by supervisors, administrators or the general public without running the risk of distorting the very goals reformers seek to achieve.

Models, methods and techniques are symptoms of basic assumptions. Without change in basic assumptions, reforms go round and round the same loops forever refining the status quo. A self renewing system calls for basic change in goals, assumptions and processes. With those in hand, intelligent professionals can find or invent appropriate techniques to implement them in practice.

Some Broad Parameters For Person-centered, Self-renewing

Schools

In light of the trends and new understandings outlined in chapters two and three, it is possible to discern some broad outlines for the kinds of schools we need, even if we cannot describe them with great precision. The changing needs of society and young people, the nature of the future for which we hope to prepare our youth and modern conceptions of healthy growth and learning all point to the need for person- centered schools and teachers. Here are a few of the broad parameters about which person-centered schools must be concerned:

Closer Relation To Student Needs

The importance of student need plays little part in the overall structure of traditional schools or in the teaching strategies of most classrooms. Student motivation, commitment and responsibility are constant problems for teachers and administrators. Many good teachers are sensitive to the needs of their students simply because they like kids. Nevertheless, they remain unable to utilize much of this valuable information because they do not know how or because the constraints of traditional school organization and practice makes relating learning to need an almost impossible task. Bigness, commonality, grouping, and the industrial model leave little room for concern with student needs. To implement what we know about need and motivation requires, at the very least, individualized instruction, smaller, autonomous schools and teachers keenly aware of the importance of need in the learning process and free to experiment with ways to put such knowledge to work.

Because traditional schools must cover a standardized curriculum, they are forever having to lay on requirements, willy nilly, whether students are in receptive attitudes or not. Since the curriculum offered is rarely consonant with the existing needs of students, teachers must contrive artificial needs to learn like grades, or a wide variety of rewards or punishments to motivate learning. This works for some students and so encourages teachers to keep trying harder in the same directions. Result: learnings that don't stick beyond tomorrow's quiz, bored or lackadaisical students, and a widespread student belief that school is a game to be played with the least possible disruption to one's personal life. Most schools are drab uninteresting institutions and often feel like pressure cookers with seething forces barely held in restraint. It is no accident that many of today's students fail to exert themselves, complain that schools "are so irrelevant" or decide to drop out at the high school level. Children in lower grades do not have that option. They must live with the system no matter what.

The message for reform is clear. Our schools are out of touch with student needs. This failure is important, not simply because motivation is needed for learning. The fulfillment of student needs is, itself, a necessary factor in human growth and development. A major purpose of schools is to meet the developing needs of students and to help students learn how to do it more effectively for themselves. To meet student needs and help them find fulfilling new ones, requires person- centered teachers who are close enough to students to be aware of student needs and skillful at relating needs to the learning process.

Challenging Young People.

In recent years we have been treated to study after study calling attention to "the deplorable lack of information and skill" of American students as compared to those of other countries. While many of the conclusions drawn from these statistics and the remedies suggested are seriously in error, the fact remains, our students are not being sufficiently challenged by the current system. Too many are bored, content to just get by or choose to avoid rigorous classes and programs. Those numbers do not include the drop outs or the ones who give up altogether. The facts are indisputable; we are failing to challenge too many of our young people. It is time we applied what we know of the dynamics of challenge and threat to the construction of person-centered schools, programs and classroom practices.

We have seen in the previous chapter the crucial role in learning played by the experience of challenge and threat. People learn best, when they are challenged and free from the experience of threat. What challenges or threatens students is a highly individual matter having to do with their unique ways of perceiving what is happening to them. To avoid threatening learners and to assure challenging them, schools and teachers must be keenly aware of what is going on in the private worlds of their students on one hand and cognizant of the probable effects of their own behavior on the other. Teachers need to be empathic, tuned in to the ways things seem from the points of view of their students. Instruction needs to be individualized, adapted to the needs and readiness of pupils. Educators have long recognized the need for individualized instruction but, for the most part, have been weaned away from tackling the question vigorously. It is time we made serious efforts to implement this vital factor.

Learning As Personal Meaning.

Most schools have developed the mechanics for providing students with information to a fine art. With the use of modern electronic equipment we are able to process information faster, in greater quantity and more attractively or dramatically than ever before. But exposure to information is only the first half of the learning equation. The more important aspect lies in helping students discover its personal meaning. That calls for strategy and tactics unfamiliar to many teachers and administrators who have been trained to value objectivity and the manipulation of forces approach to practice. As we have seen, learning is not an objective phenomenon. It is a warm, highly personal, human, subjective, largely social process. This new understanding of the nature of learning is so fundamental that it calls for reform in every aspect of the system, especially in the classroom and interrelationships of students and teachers.

For generations schools have operated from a manipulation of forces assumption about learning. We have designed our schools and planned our curricula and programs from that frame of reference. Most of our schools and teachers are committed to a mechanical view of learning rather than an experiential one. Teachers are indoctrinated with the manipulation of forces viewpoint and taught to use it in their professional practice. Accordingly, they are preoccupied with content, subject matter and teaching techniques. A few students thrive on these conditions. Most others conform to the process and turn in tolerable but less than optimal performance. A sizeable proportion fall far below their capacities because the process is so far out of sync with their needs and abilities. Inadequate assumptions lead to inadequate results. We have lived and worked with the manipulation of forces assumption too long. It is time to close the gap and update the concepts of learning upon which the system rests. To bring our schools into closer accord with the best we know about behavior and learning, schools must become person-centered. They must be made brain compatible and user friendly.

Promoting Positive Views Of Self.

If we accept the findings of scholars and researchers about health and fulfillment, we have still further reasons to seek more person-centered schools. Modern perceptual-experiential psychology has shown the overwhelming importance of the self concept in human behavior. People behave according to how things seem to them, especially how they see themselves and how they see the world they must confront. What people believe about themselves is involved in every behavior, even the simplest. We know, for example, that what students believe about themselves has vital effects upon abilities to learn. That fact, in itself, should be enough to make the developing self concepts of students a major concern for education and reform.

What students believe about themselves or other people has not been widely accepted as appropriate objectives for education. Schools for the most part have shied away from such aspects of student growth and concentrated upon academic and curricular concerns. The system is preoccupied with objectivity, curriculum and things. Students are often treated as objects to be molded or infused with what has been determined to be "necessary and desirable" information. Positive views of self are characteristic of healthy, responsible human beings and the development of positive selves must become a high priority objective for public schools.

Fortunately, the creation of positive self concepts is not dependent upon budgets, supplies, buildings or equipment. They are learned from experience and from interactions with others. To determine what is needed to produce such concepts we need only ask, "How can a person feel liked unless somebody likes her?", "How can a boy feel wanted unless someone wants him?", "How can a girl feel acceptable unless someone accepts her?", "How can students feel able unless somewhere they have some success?" or "How can a person feel he/she is a person of dignity and integrity unless someone treats him/her so" In the answers we find to such questions we will find important guidelines for the actions required to create more person-centered schools.

The Fallacy Of Failure.

It is widely assumed both in and out of educational circles that failure is good for people, that it provides excellent experiences for learning and motivation. Nothing could be further from the truth. Failure is far more often destructive to personality and motivation. Research demonstrates that supremely healthy persons see themselves in positive ways. Such perceptions of self are the consequence of success experience, not failure. We might compare the experience of failure, psychologically, with disease, physiologically. Disease represents a failure of the physical organism to cope. Now, we do not say about disease, "Let us give this child all the diseases we can to help him grow strong and healthy". Instead, we say, "Let us keep this child from getting disease just as long as we possibly can". Alternatively, we say, "Let us give this child a success experience with the disease. Let us give him an inoculation or vaccination against it". Success experience with a weakened form of the disease, strengthens the child to deal with the real thing if it comes along. Success strengthens persons; failure weakens them. The best guarantee we have that a person will be successful in the future is that he/she has been successful in the past. The implication is clear. We need person-centered schools to foster positive views of self.

What Are Person-centered Schools?

To bring our educational system up to date with modern conceptions of brain function, learning, motivation, student growth and development and the future toward which we are heading calls for self renewing, person-centered schools. If this is so, it follows that educational reform must concentrate upon encouraging the development of thousands of alternative person-centered schools. Instead of attempting to change the system from the top down by the imposition of laid on solutions, it will be necessary to seek reform from the bottom up through the involvement of front line workers tackling educational problems from up to date assumptions. This has the further advantage of assuring a feeling of ownership of reforms by those responsible for carrying them out. Out of such dynamic groups adapting modern concepts to the education of local youth, education will be able to meet the needs of youth more efficiently. The cumulative effect of such programs will reform the system more effectively and surely than current efforts and will keep the system engaged in self renewal at the same time.

From this point of view the task of educational reformers, whether in legislatures, school boards, parent organizations or the upper echelons of school administration will be to facilitate the development and innovative functioning of alternative person-centered schools. The task will not be easy for the proposal confronts many deep seated traditions and the frustrating inertia of bureaucracies. In view of the widespread failure of reform efforts from the top down, the reach for reform from the bottom up through the development of a system of alternative schools seems a necessary way to go. The need to achieve reform through self renewing alternative schools has also been advocated by leaders in the profession as is apparent from studies like, A Nation At Risk (1983) and from people like President Futrell of the National Education Association (1989) or President Shanker of the American Federation Of Teachers (1990).

Most schools on the current scene are essentially curriculum oriented. In general, their primary goal is for students to acquire a prescribed curriculum or skills. Teachers are regarded as controllers and directors of the process, while students are treated as objects and taught the necessary curriculum. In contrast, person-centered schools are primarily focused on the learner and his/her growth and development. The role of teacher is that of facilitator instead of controller or director. Emphasis is upon process and what is happening in the learner. Teachers act as guides, helpers, friendly representatives of society.

By person-centered schools we mean, the attempt to put into active practice the best we know about the learner and the learning process. Educators on the cutting edge of reform have been experimenting with person-centered approaches to teaching and program building for many years. Teachers in many parts of the country may be found working out the implications of one or another modern concept in planning or practice. For some, this is a conscious attempt to put some aspect of person-centered thinking to work. For others, person- centered approaches creep into practice simply "because it feels right". Mostly these efforts go unheralded and unrewarded but little by little the number of person- centered practitioners grows as teachers discover it is a happier, more productive approach to their profession. Some teachers operate in person-centered fashion in the privacy of their classrooms with little or no relation to what neighboring teachers are doing. Here and there one may also encounter groups of teachers trying out person-centered ways to teach and, occasionally, one may even find whole schools moving in such directions.

There is no precise definition of what a person- centered school ought to be, just as there are no such things as right methods. Person-centered practices arise from similar basic assumptions but their implementation is necessarily adapted to the belief systems of teachers, local student bodies, educational goals, community resources and conditions. Person-centered schools are the products of like minded faculties working out philosophy and strategies appropriate for the students and circumstances they confront. Such schools are not interchangeable. Person-centeredness is not a prescription; it is a way of thinking about students, learning and goals. How it is implemented may vary widely from school to school, even class to class. One cannot successfully lift a program from one school and set it down in another expecting identical results. Person-centered schools do not lend themselves to bigness, top down management or standardization. Instead, they are unique entities, based upon some common assumptions but highly diverse in implementation.

Some Common Characteristics Of Person-centered Schools

The Implementation Of Current Thinking

While there can be no precise definition of person-centered schools, it is possible to discern a number of similar characteristics. For example, they share a common concern to implement up to date thinking about the nature of students and the learning process. None, so far as this author is aware, have attempted systematically to translate all that is currently known about these matters into practice. Instead, person- centered schools here and there have tended to experiment with one or more modern principles, seeking ways to translate them into school or classroom practice. See, for example, interest in affective education, alternative ways of grading, evaluating or promoting, concern for student needs, self concept or readiness.

The new understandings outlined in Chapters two and three provide basic assumptions for a vast array of new thinking and practice. It is probably asking too much at this point to expect any school to implement them all. Faculties, like students, have varying states of readiness to tackle new things. For some time we shall have to be content with encouraging faculties to explore those assumptions they feel ready and eager to address.

Person oriented

Generally speaking, person-centered schools are deeply concerned with the "person in the process". In addition to traditional content and subject matter, they seek ways to help students develop trustworthy values, personal beliefs and attitudes. Their curricula tend to be less rigid, more adaptable to student needs, current concerns of society and local communities. They are less dependent upon textbook adoptions and commercially produced workbooks. Instead, they make serious efforts to individualize instruction and make much use of research and library offerings, field trips, laboratories, teacher/student contrived materials and community resources for data and experience.

Process orientation

Person-centered schools are more concerned with processes than ends. That is to say, they place higher value on what is happening to students in the processes of teaching and learning than the achievement of specific information. They believe that involvement in the processes of learning is more important than knowing specific answers, that knowing how to learn is more significant than knowing "right" facts.

Flexibility

Because they are so readily adaptable to student needs, community resources and changing ideas, the structure of person-centered schools is highly flexible. They resist iron clad rules, regulations or procedures. They tend to look upon organization and methodology as tentative--current attempts to facilitate whatever goals are under exploration but continuously subject to modification or discard as goals and circumstances warrant.

Size

Person-centered schools are the inventions of like minded faculties working out their unique ways of implementing up to date assumptions within the constraints of local facilities and the needs of students. The necessity for a like minded faculty and adaptation to a given body of students places strict limits upon the size of person-centered schools. Furthermore, because innovative faculties must work in intimate contact with one another, working groups must also be small enough to foster effective communication. It follows that each person-centered school must discover its own optimum population.

Transitional Character

Because person-centered schools are continually in a state of flux as they adapt to changing ideas, goals, resources and student bodies, they tend to flourish for a time then fade off into the sunset or may be replaced by some other philosophy or program. This is a matter of much distress to reformers. It seems reasonable that when you have a good thing, you ought to keep it. Unfortunately, permanence is not conducive to innovation, change, creativity and experimentation. Person-centered schools are also the products of like minded faculties. However, faculty members, being human, notoriously change their minds, leave the organization or the community for one reason or another. This causes the best of innovative programs or schools to change or self destruct over a period of time. While, on the surface, this tenuous character of person-centered schools seem regrettable, it also guarantees a self renewing quality to the system.

A Checklist For Person-centered Schools

Many educators, as individuals or in groups, have tried their hands at describing the kinds of person- centered schools we need. Some of the best of these efforts have come from educators attached to the so called, Humanist Movement. Unfortunately these people have come under vicious attack in recent years from right wing extremists who see the movement as subversive and ungodly. They have labeled the effort, "secular humanism" and raised such an outcry against it as to drive many person-centered teachers underground. The charge, of course, is ridiculous. Person-centered schools attempt to apply to the education of youth the best that modern science can tell us about learning and growth. Furthermore, the application of science to improving our way of life is as American as apple pie. The net effect of these unfortunate misconceptions has only served to delay badly needed reforms in educational theory and practice. We cannot afford to be intimidated into rejecting some of the most promising approaches to reform that education has seen in decades.

In 1976 the Association For Supervision And Curriculum Development appointed a distinguished group of educators to a Working Group On Humanistic Education charged with the responsibility for defining humanistic education and exploring ways by which it might be evaluated. Two years later the commission published its report in a monograph entitled: Humanistic Education: Objectives and Assessment.(1978) A special task force of the ASCD Working Group composed a carefully compiled and extensively tested 100 item "Check List For Humanistic Schools (Brown,1978) for use by parents, teachers and interested public to gauge the person- centeredness of their local schools. For readers who would like to explore the nature of person-centered schools more deeply or capture the flavor of what such schools might be like, we have reprinted the Checklist in the Appendix of this volume.

Do Person-centered Schools Sacrifice Standards?

A commonly expressed fear about person-centered schools and practices is concern for what may be left out when person-centered practices are instituted. Such fears are groundless, however, for person-centeredness is not an either-or matter. It is not a soft or indulgent way of working. Because schools are student- centered and empathic does not mean they are goody goody, laissez faire or inclined to devalue traditional subject matter or standards. Quite the contrary. Person- centered approaches are designed to assure that subject matter and standards will be more fully and successfully achieved. It is offered as a more efficient way to achieve the maximum growth and development of young people,

Research clearly demonstrates that person-centered approaches result in better performance in traditional subjects and skills as measured by standardized tests in common use throughout the nation. Perhaps the most comprehensive of these studies have been made by David Aspy, Flora Roebuck and their colleagues in the National Consortium for Humanistic Education. In their two books, A Lever Long Enough (Aspy,1976) and Kids Don't Learn From Teachers They Don't Like (Aspy,1977) the authors present research evidence from 42 states and 7 foreign countries clearly demonstrating that; not only will subject matter gains be significantly higher with person-centered teaching, but there will also be greater gains in intelligence measures, less drop outs, absenteeism and discipline problems as well. The authors suggest that we can no longer afford the inefficiencies of traditional approaches.

The person-centered movement is no cock eyed ideal or flash in the pan. It is a firmly grounded, logical, necessary, even inevitable, attempt to apply the best we know from biological, psychological and future oriented science to education. It is a response to changing demands of society and the times we live in. Applying the findings of research to practical affairs is one of the things that has made our nation great. The Person- centered movement in education attempts to do just that for education. It is also an expression in education of a world wide shift in human thought. There are comparable humanist movements in philosophy, theology, psychology, anthropology, medicine and political science. The wonder is that it has taken so long to get around to it in our public schools.

Alternative Schools And Reform

To avoid recurrence of a system so out of touch as our current one, today's reform efforts cannot be content with a one shot approach to the problem. We need a system with built in provisions for self renewal continuously engaged in the exploration of ideas, design of innovations and experimentation at every level. The establishment of thousands of person-centered alternative schools is one way to meet that objective. Current emphasis upon bigness, commonality, the industrial model, manipulation of forces thinking and top down approaches to reform must give way to the formation of person-centered schools staffed by like minded faculties and the facilitation of their operations. The task will be difficult for the necessary strategies depart very sharply from existing philosophy, practice and long standing tradition.

Fortunately, we do not need to start from scratch in this new conception of reform. The number of possibilities for exploration and adaptation to be drawn from the seven principles of learning outlined in Chapter 3 is mind boggling. There are enough to keep us busy for at least a decade. Additional fascinating assumptions are being proposed almost daily from modern explorations in such fields as human development, motivation and learning, perceptual-experiential psychologies, brain research, psychotherapy, group process, health and self actualization. The problem is choosing which assumptions are most worth exploring for a particular faculty or community. Similarly, thousands of techniques for implementing assumptions are available in the gold mine of practices invented by good teachers in many parts of the country. Additional sources of ideas and practices can be found in the innovative programs of alternative schools already established in many communities. We have hardly begun to tap these rich stores of hypotheses for innovative thought and action. The references at the end of this and later chapters are but a small sample of some fertile sources of ideas for persons interested in reform and innovation through person-centered alternative schools.

Notes And References

General references:

Bredekamp, S.1989. Developmentally appropriate practice. Washington, D.C. National Association for the Education Of Young Children.

Educational Commission of the States, 1985 Reconnecting youth: The next stage of reform. Denver, Co. Education and Business Advisory Commission.

Michaels, K. 1988. "Caution: Second wave reform taking place" Educational Leadership, 45, 3-4.

Miles, M. and Hubermann, M, 1984. Innovation up close. New York, Praeger.

National Commission on Excellence In Education. 1983. A Nation at risk; the imperative for educational reform. Washington, D.C. Government Printing Office.

Sizers, T. 1984. Horace's compromise: The dilemma of the American high school. Boston, Ma. Houghton-Mifflin.

Timar, T and Kirk, D. 1989 "Educational reform in the 1980"s: Lessons from the states". Phi Delta Kappan, 70, 504-511.

66

On learning:

A.S.C.D. 1969. Humanizing the secondary school. Alexandria, Va. Association for Supervision and Curriculum Development.

Baron, J and Sternberg, R. 1987.Teaching thinking skills: Theory and practice. New York, Freeman.

Combs, A. 1985. Helping Relationships: Basic Concepts For the Helping Professions Boston, MA Allyn and Bacon.

Della-Dora, D. and Blanchard, L. 1979. Moving toward self-directed learning. Alexandria, Va. Association for Supervision and Curriculum Development.

Knowles, M. 1975. Self directed learning: A guide for learners and teachers. New York. Association Press.

Welch, I. and Usher, R. 1978. "Humanistic education: The discovery of personal meaning". Colorado Journal of Educational Research, 17, 17-23.

Rogers, C. 1967. "The interpersonal relationship in the facilitation of learning". IN Humanizing education: the person in the process Alexandria, Va. Association for Supervision and Curriculum Development.

On the self in person-centered schools:

Canfield, J. and Wells, H. 1976. 100 ways to enhance self concept in the classroom. Englewood Cliffs, N.J. Prentice Hall.

Hamachek, D. 1970 The self in growth, teaching and learning Englewood Cliffs, N.J. Prentice Hall.

Purkey, W. 1970. Self concept and school achievement. Englewood Cliffs, N.J. Prentice Hall.

On person-centered schools:

Boyer, E. 1988. "A generational imperative: Educate all our children." The Generational Journal, 1988, 1-5.

Combs, A. 1978 Humanistic education: The person in the process. Alexandria, Va. Association for Supervision and Curriculum Development.

Combs, A. 1988. "Is there a future for humanistic person-centered education?" Person-centered Review, 3, 96-103.

Gregory, T. and Smith, G. 1987.High schools as communities: The small school reconsidered. Bloomington, IN, Phi Delta Kappa.

Glasser, W. 1975. Schools without failure. New York, Harper and Row.

Holt, J. 1988. How children fail, New York. Dell Publishers.

Holt, J. 1989. Learning all the time. Reading, Ma. Addison-Wesley.

Howard, E. et. al. 1987. "Handbook for conducting school climate improvement projects" Bloomington, IN. Phi Delta Kappa Education Foundation.

Howe, L. and Howe, M. 1975. Personalizing education: Values clarification and beyond. New York, Hart Publishers.

Jeter,.J. 1980 Approaches to individualizing instruction. Alexandria, Va. Association for Supervision and Curriculum Development.

Johnson, D. and Johnson, R. 1975. Learning together and alone. Englewood Cliffs, N.J., Prentice Hall.

On the need for person-centered alternatives:

Aspy, D. and Roebuck, F. 1976. A lever long enough. Washington, D.C. The National Consortium for Humanistic Education.

Aspy, D. and Roebuck, F. 1977. Kids don't learn from teachers they don't like. Amherst, Ma. Human Resources Development Press.

Brown, D. 1978. "A checklist for humanistic schools" IN ASCD, Humanistic education: Objectives and assessment, Alexandria, Va. Association for Supervision and curriculum Development.

Combs, A. 1981. "Humanistic education: Too tender for a tough world?" Phi Delta Kappan, 1981,446-449.

Futrell, M. 1989. "Mission not accomplished: Educational reform in retrospect" Phi Delta Kappan, 71, 8-14.

68

McDaniel, T. 1989. "Demilitarizing public education: School reform in the era of George Bush" Phi Delta Kappan, 71,15-18.

Raywid, M. 1987. "Public Choice, yes; Vouchers, no!". Phi Delta Kappan 1987, 766.

Raywid, M. 1984. "Synthesis of research on schools of choice." Educational Leadership, April, 1984, 71-78.

Shanker, A. "The end of the traditional model of schooling---and a proposal for using incentives to restructure our public schools" Phi Delta Kappan, 71,344-358

CHAPTER 5

SOME OVERALL STRATEGIES

To make the kind of changes required for effective reforms in our current system requires much more than dabbling with regulations, plants, equipment or techniques. Whatever we decide to try must fit the goals we seek, the principles we hold dear, the environment in which they are to be used and the persons who are expected to carry out the plan. Beginning from basic assumptions about learning, we have established a need for person centered, self renewing alternative schools. To achieve such a system two overall strategies are available to us: a closed system and an open one.

Each of these systems represents a frame of reference for approaching the problem of change and each has implications extending into all phases of education, including the operation of person-centered schools and classrooms and the strategies employed to bring them into being. A commitment to one or the other strategy also commits teachers, administrators and ancillary personnel to a whole series of further stands with respect to philosophy, goals, curriculum, administration, values and teacher-pupil relationships.

Closed And Open Systems

Closed system thinking begins with some clearly defined objective, selects the machinery or techniques needed to reach it, puts the plan into operation, then assesses the outcome to determine if, indeed, the objective was achieved. This is the approach one would use in establishing an itinerary, producing a product in industry or teaching a child an arithmetic function. Closed system thinking has been very useful in many aspects of our technological society. It also has great appeal to legislators, business people, school boards, administrators and parents. It is a way of thinking they are used to. Indeed, it seems so logical, straightforward and business-like that few people ever stop to question it. It is the preferred approach to educational problems we have relied upon for many years. The manipulation of forces frame of reference is an expression of closed system thinking and most attempts at reform over the past forty years have been conceived in that mode.

Open systems, on the other hand, often operate without clear cut goals or objectives. One confronts a problem then searches for solutions--the nature of which cannot be clearly discerned in the beginning. This is the approach that counselors use in helping a client explore a personal problem. It is also the system used by a legislature in debating an issue, in a laboratory seeking a cure for cancer, by an artist producing a painting or in modern "discovery" methods of teaching. Unfortunately, open system thinking is far less understood in our society and consequently much less frequently employed. Here and there it is being used by teachers, primarily in classroom settings. It is extremely important for education, especially for the problem of educational reform.

To contrast these two approaches let us imagine their application to a problem of our inner cities; improving the lot of citizens in the ghetto. Approaching the problem from a closed system frame of reference, a social work administrator sitting in his office conceived an exciting plan. Why not have the city's luncheon clubs "Adopt a block" in the ghetto and provide the means to upgrade a neighborhood? Broaching the plan to several service clubs, he was delighted to get their assent. With commitments in hand he met with the people on the block to be adopted and enthusiastically set forth the proposal. He was totally unprepared for the reaction. These "chosen" people felt demeaned and insulted by the proposition. Angrily they told the well meaning administrator to "Take your plan and shove it! We don't need no help from whitey!"

Some years later another community worker operating from an open system approach had more success. She joined the neighborhood group and after some months suggested, "Why don't we get some of the rich folks in the city to subsidize our neighborhood ?" The people of the neighborhood were intrigued with the idea. After much debate the plan was enthusiastically adopted. Instead of "Adopt a block", they called their project "Block Power!" and a majority of the neighborhood got into the act. A committee was formed to select appropriate projects and another committee laid their proposal before several of the city's service clubs. The project was approved and put into action with much success.

Whichever frame of reference is chosen as the basis for change, it inevitably commits the chooser to a whole series of consequents bearing upon a wide variety of circumstances and relationships. Figure 3 presents some of these in chart form for each system. Let us examine them in greater detail.

Figure 3

Open And Closed Systems of Thinking in Reform

Topic	Closed System	Open System
The focus	Behavior management, control, or manipulation Based on Behavioristic psychology	Process oriented-facilitating conditions Based on Perceptual-experiential psychology
The leader	Expert diagnostician Total responsibility Precise goals or skills Director, manipulator of forces and outcome	Guide, helper Responsibility shared Broader goals Consultant, aid, facilitator
Curriculum	Oughts and shoulds Right answers Prepare for world Specific goals, grades and evaluation	Process goals Creation of conditions Problem centered Fill needs, create new ones
Techniques	Industrial Competition and evaluation valued Administration dominant Emphasis on goal achievement	Personal growth model Cooperative effort Problem centered Many group decisions Emphasis on intelligent problem solving
Philosophy	Control and direction Great man concept Doubts about motivation	Growth philosophy Democratic Trust in human organism
Participants	Passive Leader seen as enemy Dependent Lack commitment Conformity valued Endurance of stress	Active, responsible Leader seen as helper Participate in decisions Involved Creativity valued Concern for others
Values	Simple skills Ends clearly known Conditions for change clearly in leader's hands	Broad goals Ends not precisely predictable Humane concerns prominent

72

The Focus

A closed system focuses attention on behavioral outcomes defined in the clearest possible terms. Thereafter, the most efficient methods for achieving them are formulated and placed in operation. The system's psychological basis comes from the manipulation of forces frame of reference found in behavioral psychologies. Emphasis is upon the management of stimuli or consequents to produce preplanned outcomes. Teachers and administrators operating in this mode are concerned with management and control of persons or the forces impinging upon them. Motivation is defined as; what leaders do to participants to induce them to move toward clearly defined objectives. Goals may be established by the participants. More often they are defined by experts, established policies, the curriculum, or by administrators. The "behavioral objectives" movement of the 70's and 80's was a prime example of the application of closed system thinking to educational reform.

Open system thinking is a process oriented frame of reference. It is especially applicable to situations wherein hoped for outcomes cannot be precisely defined in advance. Leaders concentrate instead upon creating conditions conducive for the exploration of problems and the mutual search for solutions. Open system thinking finds its psychological base in perceptual-experiential psychology. It is concerned, not only with behavior, but also with attitudes, feelings, beliefs, values or the perceptions that produce behavior. The processes of change are advanced by encouraging participants in the search for solutions and by facilitating optimal conditions for the processes of exploration and discovery. Motivation in this system is seen as an internal matter having to do with participant needs, likes, dislikes, goals and aspirations.

The Leader

In a closed system all responsibility for making sure that ends are properly achieved is lodged in the leader. The process is similar to the familiar medical model. One goes to the doctor and states her problem. The doctor then diagnoses the situation, determines the goals to be achieved and writes a prescription for the patient who is expected to carry out the doctor's orders. Responsibility for control and direction is almost exclusively in the hands of the leader with the participant in a passive or subservient role. The model is also found in the structure of modern industry, the military and many other institutions. In a closed system the task of the leader is to assure progress toward preconceived goals. To do this well, leaders must be expert diagnosticians who know at any moment what is going on and where events must be channeled next. This places almost total responsibility on the leader both to define goals and for the achievement of them. The leader's role is that of director or manager responsible for the manipulation of forces or consequents so that preconceived ends will be achieved.

Open systems have a quite different locus of responsibility. Since end products are not precisely known in advance, responsibility for outcomes is shared by all who are engaged in confronting the problem. Because more people share in the discussion, more possible solutions are formulated. The emphasis in open systems is on participation and sharing of power and decision making. This jointly shared responsibility removes a great burden from the leaders. They do not <u>have</u> to be right. The role of the leader is not manager or director, but helper or facilitator. His/her expertise lies in the advancement of processes and the creation of conditions for change. The leader serves as facilitator to aid, assist, help or serve as consultant in an on-going process of exploration and discovery.

The Curriculum

The curriculum, seen from the perspective of a closed system, consists of a body of knowledge, subject matter, information or skills to be inculcated in students. These are couched in terms of "oughts" or "shoulds" generally defined by society, legislators, administrators, supervisors, teachers or parents as important objectives of schooling. Most teaching revolves around these objectives. Forces like evaluation, competition, grades and various forms of reward and punishment are instituted to assure maximum achievement by students.

Viewed from an open system the curriculum is also concerned with helping students acquire knowledge and skills for effective citizenship. Goals, however, are much less precisely articulated with many opportunities for diversity and individual choice. Much of the curriculum is also likely to be defined in process terms as --problem solving, creativity, responsibility, learning how to learn, or in broader less precisely defined subject matter objectives. Because goals are broader and more personal, cooperation is more likely to be stressed and evaluation or grading is emphasized less. Open systems place greater emphasis upon filling individual needs and discovering new ones.

Techniques And Methods

The focus of closed systems is on management and control. Consequently methods are likely to be patterned after industrial or medical models with control in the hands of "experts" or bosses intent upon the achievement of manifest objectives. Techniques tend to concentrate on things or forces designed to channel behavior toward desired ends. Competition and evaluative techniques are highly valued in such a system with much concern for goal achievement, standards and discipline. Administrative hierarchies tend to be sharply drawn with clear distinctions between leaders and followers.

Open system methods follow a growth model. Like growing a healthy plant, one places the seed in the best soil to be found, surrounds the plant with the best possible growing conditions and lets it grow. Open systems concentrate upon processes, on facilitating optimal conditions for participant explorations and discovery. Cooperation between participants and leaders is valued and group decisions are frequently manifest. The emphasis is less upon right answers and more on intelligent problem solving.

Philosophy

Closed system emphasis upon control, direction and the determination of goals by leaders leads, in the extreme, to a "great man" concept. Such a philosophy seeks a "great man" who knows where people should go so that he/she or designated subordinates, can assure that they get there. The position has doubts about the adequacy of human motivation and capacities and seeks people who know to lead and instruct those who do not.

Operating from a growth philosophy, open system thinking begins with a basic trust in the human organism and concentrates on creating conditions to facilitate operation of human resources. Its approaches are essentially democratic. It recognizes the fundamental dignity and integrity of the organism and seeks to implement the belief that, "when people are free, they can find their own best ways".

Effects On Participants

Because most decisions are made by the leaders in a closed system of thinking, participants tend to be passive, doing what is expected of them. They may also become dependent upon leaders for answers and decisions. Closed systems frequently devolve into advocacy relationships in which leaders may be regarded as "the enemy" and overtly or covertly resisted. Stress and anxiety are frequent characteristics of closed systems. When people do not share in the decisions that affect their lives they tend to conform to the system, break out in rebellion, or leave the field by copping out or dropping out. They often become the victims of "learned helplessness" believing they have no control over their destinies.

In open systems, leaders are more likely to be regarded as helpers or friendly representatives of society. As a consequence, participants are more actively involved. They participate in decision making and are, therefore, more likely to be cooperative and responsible. Because more persons are involved in explorations, more possible solutions are also brought to light. Since participants "own" the process, they are more likely to commit to its decisions. With emphasis upon problem solving, open systems are also more likely to be creative than conforming. Tension levels are generally lower in open systems and participants show greater concern for one another.

Values And Use

The preceding paragraphs have delineated sharply between closed and open systems of thinking and their implications for educational practice. This is intentional in order to contrast the two positions. It should be recognized, of course, that such sharp distinctions do not ordinarily appear in daily practice. These are not either-or positions. Rather, at any moment educators may be observed to be operating in one or the other frame of reference as occasion demands. Each way of operating has important values. The point is, not to adopt one or the other position exclusively but to understand each one and to utilize each in its appropriate sphere of application.

Generally speaking, closed system thinking and management techniques can be highly useful in situations wherein: 1. outcomes can be clearly, and,2. simply defined in advance and 3. when the means to control events is firmly in the hands of the leader. The approach is especially useful in dealing with things or when the effects upon participants can be ignored. The conditions for effective use of closed systems are often present in classroom situations, especially in connection with the teaching of specific skills or precisely defined behaviors at the elementary level. They may also exist occasionally in the relationships of administrators and teachers. The effectiveness of closed system thinking rapidly disintegrates, however, as the need to cope with persons and their interactions with each other becomes more critical. Applied to the primary problems of reform these limits severely restrict the usefulness of closed system approaches.

Open system thinking will generally prove more useful for reaching the goals of educational reform. Open systems are especially relevant:
1. for the attainment of broad goals or,
2. when objectives cannot be spelled out in finite terms.
3. They also have special usefulness when we are concerned about producing some change in people's inner experience; in feelings, attitudes, beliefs, values, personal meanings or commitments. Education, as we have seen, is a people business and the problems of educational reform call for a frame of reference uniquely designed for influencing persons. While closed

system thinking will have occasional applications in the processes of reform, we are far more likely to bring about the changes we need from an open frame of reference.

Which System For Reform?

Traditional schools and classrooms are, for the most part, designed and operated from closed system thinking. Goals and curricula are clearly defined in advance with teachers who are presumed to be experts directing and controlling events. Students, in turn, are regarded as persons to be taught and are expected to cooperate in the endeavor.

Person-centered schools are called for by the changing nature of society, the future for which youth need to be prepared and most recent advances in understanding about the learner and the learning process. Implementation of such schools must rely heavily upon open system thinking both in the design of person-centered schools and the ways in which they operate. The principles of open system thinking provide important basic assumptions upon which person-centered schools may be established. They also suggest guidelines for the professional practices of teachers and administrators.

Closed system thinking results in methods of direction, control and management. It advocates top down strategies and encourages attempts to bring about reform by the manipulation of forces and preoccupation with things. Operating from a closed system of thinking, the problem of reform typically would be addressed by:

Analyzing the problem and setting goals
Consulting experts and the literature
Drawing up a plan
Assigning workers and responsibility
Attempting to control and redirect forces that seem to be bearing on
    the problem.

We have used that approach for fifty years or more with indifferent results. It is a major thesis of this book that effective reform is more likely to be achieved through the development of alternative schools organized around like minded faculties attempting to implement modern understandings about student growth and learning. The establishment and operation of such person-centered schools calls for the application of open system thinking and action. It is equally important as a basic set of guidelines for reform of the total system. Open system thinking, however, does not lend itself readily to mass application. It is generally limited to groups small enough for individuals to interact effectively with one another. Accordingly, we are confronted with a choice--a. to continue with a management strategy applicable to large numbers but a history of disappointing results or b., to adopt a more promising strategy aimed at changing people but limited to smaller units. The former gives the illusion of making a large, if inadequate, effort. The latter requires a revolutionary change in strategy that extends into every phase of American education. If we accept the necessity to approach reform from a person-centered orientation, it will require learning to work in open system fashion with and through people at every level of the system especially with teachers and their immediate supervisors.

What Makes A Good Teacher?

A second major change in overall strategy for reform is called for by new conceptions of the nature of the teaching-administering task and the qualities of effective helpers. Just as our conceptions of brain functioning, motivation, learning and the future have changed requiring widespread adaptations in education, so, also, must we change our thinking about what makes a good teacher or administrator.

Knowledge of Content and Teaching Skills

For many years we have considered good teaching primarily as a matter of knowledge of subject matter and the skill to teach it effectively. More recently we have been forced to conclude that both assumptions are faulty. No one would suggest that knowledge of subject matter is unimportant for effective teaching. Of course it is important. But knowledge alone is no guarantee of good teaching. Who has not suffered at the hands of a teacher who knew his/her subject well but was unable to teach it effectively? Subject matter is the stuff to be transmitted. Whether that happens is dependent upon the skill of teachers in facilitating the processes of learning. This is especially true for elementary teachers who must introduce children to ten or fifteen subjects, like math, science, reading, social studies, art, music, physical education, health, geography, history, spelling, writing, plus drug and sex education. For elementary teachers intensive knowledge of subject matter is far less important than understanding children and how they grow and learn. At high school and college levels where education is more specialized, the teacher's in depth knowledge of subject matter becomes more important but, even at these levels, is no guarantee of good teaching.

Methods and Good Teaching

Neither is good teaching a matter of employing "right" methods. We have seen in the previous chapter, that despite numerous attempts, research has been unable to establish any method that clearly discriminates between good and poor professional helpers. Methods are so complex and must fit so many variables that the hope of finding universal right ones is an exercise in futility. But everyone knows from personal experience as a student that there are differences in the quality of teaching or administering. If the difference is not in knowledge or methods, what is it?

The Crucial Character of Belief Systems

For many years we have considered teaching as a mechanical operation of doing the right things at the right time and in the right ways. Accordingly, reform efforts have been preoccupied with methods and things. Recent researches on good and poor teaching demonstrate, however, that effective teaching is not a direct function of knowledge or methods. It is a matter of attitudes and beliefs. That is to say, good teaching is dependent upon teacher belief systems, especially, what teachers believe about themselves, their students, their subject matter and their profession. This understanding changes our whole conception of teaching, of how we must approach the matter of teacher education, of facilitating the teacher's task in the classroom and what we must do to bring about effective reform.

Good Helper Research

A whole series of studies on good and poor helpers, including teachers and administrators, has recently demonstrated that good practitioners can be clearly distinguished from poor ones on the nature of their belief systems. (See chapter notes), People behave according to the nature of their perceptions, feelings, attitudes or beliefs. Teachers too. What makes a good teacher, therefore, is a function of the teacher's beliefs about self, other people, the purposes of teaching and the personal tactics and strategies for achieving goals to which a teacher ascribes. Effective teachers are persons who have learned to use themselves as effective instruments to carry out their own and society's purposes. They have learned to see themselves, their students, subject matter and the teaching task in clear and accurate terms. Such perceptions or beliefs serve the teacher as personal theories or guidelines for thinking and acting. They make it possible to confront complex events and respond instantaneously with appropriate and effective solutions. Good teachers are not mechanics; they are creative, professional persons responding to their tasks as thinking problem solvers. How well they are able to do that is dependent upon the belief systems they have acquired in the course of training and experience.

Here is a summary of the findings derived from eighteen studies on good and poor practitioners in the helping professions (references in chapter notes):

1. Good teachers and administrators are person-centered. That is to say, they are sensitive or empathic to how things seem to the persons they work with. They are tuned in to the personal meanings or perceptions of those they hope to teach and use this data to guide their own thinking and action. Poor practitioners, on the other hand, are preoccupied with how things look to themselves. Since people behave according to how things seem to them, the empathy characteristic of good helpers keeps them in touch with the fundamental data required to carry out their functions effectively. They are people, rather than things oriented, more concerned with what is happening in their students or colleagues than with rules, regulations, mechanics or the minutiae of their jobs. They are also the kinds of persons needed to conceive and operate person-centered schools and programs.

2. Good helpers see themselves in positive ways. They see themselves as liked, wanted, acceptable, able persons of dignity and integrity. Poor ones do not. Because they see themselves in positive ways, good teachers and administrators carry themselves with assurance and approach their tasks expecting to be successful and usually are. Such concepts of self provide the confidence and security to confront problems, to innovate and experiment with creative solutions. Feeling sure of themselves, good practitioners behave with confidence and students and colleagues in turn respond to them with trust and respect, making their efforts more likely to succeed. Message for reform: whatever denigrates the profession or the self concepts of teachers or administrators is destructive to reform. Instead, efforts at reform will need to appreciate and enhance the profession in general and the self esteem of its practitioners in particular.

3. Effective teachers and administrators see the people they work with in positive ways. They see them as trustworthy, friendly, able, persons of dignity and integrity. Poor helpers have grave doubts about the character and capacities of those they work with. Such attitudes are destructive of reform. Teachers are the front line operators on whom the processes of reform must depend. If you do not believe that people are able---you don't dare let them! If you do not believe people are trustworthy, you dare not grant them responsibility. Any reform dependent upon the cooperation of others must begin from positive beliefs about those it hopes to influence. The self renewing, person-centered schools required for effective reform will need teachers and administrators with positive views of students and the people who teach them.

4. The behavior of good practitioners is motivated by their beliefs

about purposes and goals. For example, good helpers tend to have opening, freeing goals and purposes rather than controlling, restraining ones. These are also the kinds of qualities required for person-centered schools and programs. Poor helpers are unclear or confused about their purposes. To break loose from the status quo calls for teachers and administrators ready and willing to innovate and experiment with new assumptions and ways of working. Freeing, opening, broadening attitudes are essential for creativity and the innovative, experimental goals of self renewing reforms.

5. The belief systems of good practitioners tend to be self revealing rather than self concealing. Good teachers and administrators are essentially authentic. Their behavior springs from deeply held feelings and beliefs. It is not put on or acted. This applies as well to the strategies and methods they employ. Poor helpers tend to be self concealing. Good practitioners operate in the courage of their convictions. They utilize methods that fit the students and circumstances they work with and their own belief systems even if such methods are quite different from those around them. Such personal integrity and willingness to risk is essential both for effective reform and for participation in person-centered schools.

Some Implications For Reform Strategy

For truly person-centered schools effective teaching requires truly professional people, teachers and administrators who can handle the multifarious aspects and demands of students, curriculum and learning in effective and creative ways. Confining teachers to the straightjackets of canned curricula, cook book approaches to technique or required methodologies is a shameful waste and inefficiency. It also demoralizes the profession. Teachers must be free to behave as true professionals, encouraged to exercise fully their knowledge and skills with a minimum of interference. The final responsibilities for reform lie with them. Every attempt must, therefore, be made to facilitate their operation as true professionals. This includes intimate involvement in educational planning and decision making, not only in their classrooms but in the larger system as well.

To bring about change at the front line is a threefold task:
1. To make significant information readily available to teachers and administrators,
2. to facilitate the incorporation of new concepts into their belief systems,
3. to free teachers and administrators to translate new concepts into action in their own professional settings.

Teachers and administrators are far smarter and more creative than they are given credit for. They can and they will change classrooms if encouraged and freed to do so. To approach reform through self renewing, person-centered schools will require enlistment or development of high quality teachers and administrators capable of working effectively in open system ways.

On The Larger Scene

Understanding effective performance as a consequence of the belief systems of teachers and administrators has far reaching implications for reform. For one thing, it helps us comprehend why so many of our well intended efforts have failed to pay off. It explains why the top down, things oriented attempts of the past fifty years have proven so disappointing: those efforts addressed the wrong targets. They concentrate upon things instead of people. They failed to produce basic changes in the belief systems of those on the front line. With more accurate knowledge about the dynamics of behavior we should be able to improve upon our chances for reform.

To be more effective, whatever is done for reform must produce some change in the belief systems of the participants. Reform efforts must become people oriented. Unfortunately, (or perhaps, fortunately), people's beliefs are not open to direct manipulation and cannot be changed without some degree of personal involvement of the responsible persons. This changes the whole focus of reform efforts from things to people and calls for strategies designed to facilitate change in personal meaning. That, in turn, calls for open, rather than closed system thinking and practice.

Approaching reform from an open system philosophy will no doubt be met with dismay in many quarters. Some will say, "But we don't have time. We've got to get faster results." What is the alternative? We can do more of what we have been doing. We can try harder at the old stand, throw more money at the problem with little hope of greatly improving our track record. Or, we can recognize the need to change old assumptions and get to work from more promising frames of reference. People do not change quickly and tooling up for a new approach will, of course, take time. But not as long as one might think. The theoretical bases are largely in place in what we now know about brain function, learning, motivation, self fulfillment and group dynamics and the nature of the future our children face. There are also methods and processes galore from which to choose technology. What is critically needed is to free the players to make use of available knowledge and to translate it into action.

Open system thinking and a person-centered approach to reform requires recognition of the vital role of teachers and first level administrators, encouraging them to confront today's problems, and facilitating efforts to find new and more promising approaches. Experimentation and innovation must be inspired, supported and applauded in classrooms, departments, and schools throughout the system. Teachers, as individuals, in teams or schools, must be encouraged and freed to tackle the problems before them in the light of up to date assumptions.

Unfortunately, we do not have a ready cadre of teachers and administrators ready and willing to invent and operate the person-centered alternative schools we need. Most currently employed personnel were trained in manipulation of forces, closed system thinking and have accumulated most of their experience in the very schools we now must reform. They will not take easily to the demands and expectations of open system, person-centered ways of operating. It is a difficult thing for anyone to make fundamental changes in thinking or well established habits of acting. Many teachers will not be able to make the necessary adjustments. Even for those who embrace new thinking the path will be frustrating and painful, strewn with mistakes and false starts. It will also take time to change long standing beliefs and ways of working. Recruiting teachers and administrators to the task and keeping them at it long enough to experience success will require tolerance from their communities, skilled human relationships on the part of supervisors and administrators and a new professionalism all round. Our failures are not from a dearth of ideas. We are awash with concepts and possibilities. Rather, our problem is; how to select or invent appropriate reforms to try and how to get them used by the people who must put them to work. People must own the problems and the solutions required if reform is to be truly effective.

Notes And References

General references:

Atkin, J. 1989. "Can educational research keep pace with educational reform?" Phi Delta Kappan 71, 200-206

Cawelti, G. 1989. "Designing high schools for the future." Educational Leadership, 47, 30-35.

Crowell, S. 1989. "A new way of thinking: The challenge of the future". Educational Leadership. 47, 60-63.

ECS Task Force on Education for economic growth. 1983. Action for excellence: A comprehensive plan to improve our nation's schools. Washington, D.C. Educational Commission of the States.

Fullan, M. 1982. The meaning of education change. New York, Teachers College Press.

Naisbitt, J. 1982. Megatrends. New York, Basic Books.
Sarason, S. 1982. The culture of the school and the problem of change. Boston, Ma. Allyn and Bacon.

Schlesinger, B. 1986. "The challenge of change". New York Times Magazine, July 27, 1989, 20-21.

Timar, T. 1989. 1989. "The politics of school restructuring". Phi Delta Kappan, 71,264-275.

Research on good and poor helpers:

Aspy, D. and Buhler, K. 1975. "The effect of teachers inferred self concepts upon student achievement." Journal of Educational Research, 47, 386-389.

Benton, J. 1964. Perceptual characteristics of Episcopal pastors. Doctoral dissertation, Gainesville, FL. University of Florida.

Brown, R. 1970. A study of the perceptual organization of elementary and secondary "Outstanding Young Educators". Doctoral dissertation, Gainesville, FL. University of Florida.

Choy, C. 1969. The relationship of college teacher effectiveness to conceptual systems of orientation and perceptual organization Doctoral dissertation, Greeley, CO. University of Northern Colorado.

Combs, A. 1969. Florida studies in the helping professions Social Science Monograph #37, Gainesville FL. University of Florida Press.

Combs, A. 1982. A personal approach to teaching: Beliefs that make a difference. Boston, Allyn and Bacon.

Combs, A. and Soper, D. 1963. "The perceptual organization of effective counselors.". Journal of Counseling Psychology, 10, 222-227.

Dedrick, C. 1972. The relationship between perceptual characteristics and effective teaching at the junior college level. Doctoral dissertation, Gainesville, FL University of Florida.

84

Doyle, E. 1969. The relationship between college teacher effectiveness and inferred characteristics of the adequate personality. Doctoral dissertation, Greeley, CO. University of Northern Colorado.

Dunning, D. 1982. A study of the perceptual characteristics of Episcopal priests identified and not identified as most effective. Doctoral dissertation, Santa Barbara, CA. The Fielding Institutes.

Gooding, C. 1964, An observational analysis of the perceptual organization of effective teachers. Doctoral dissertation, Gainesville, FL. University of Florida.

Harvey, O. 1970. "Belief and behavior: Some implications for education." The Science Teacher, 37,10-14.

Jennings, G. 1973. The relationship between perceptual characteristics and effective advising of university housing para-professional residence assistants Doctoral dissertation, Gainesville, FL. University of Florida.

Koffman, R. 1975. A comparison of the perceptual organizations of outstanding and randomly selected teachers in open and closed classrooms. Doctoral dissertation, Anherst, MA. University of Massachusetts.

O'Roark, A. 1974. A comparison of perceptual characteristics of elected legislators and public school counselors identified as most and least effective. Doctoral dissertation, Gainesville, FL. University of Florida.

Usher, R. 1966. The relationships of perceptions of self, others and the helping task to certain measures of college faculty effectiveness. Doctoral dissertation, Gainesville, FL. University of Florida.

Vonk, H. 1970. The relationship of teacher effectiveness to perceptions of self and teacher purposes. Doctoral dissertation, Gainesville, FL. University of Florida

CHAPTER 6

FACILITATING CHANGE

To bring about the person-centered schools we need, it will be necessary to challenge teachers and administrators to get involved in the reform movement. As we have seen in Chapter 4, people feel challenged when they are confronted with problems that seem important to them and which they feel able to solve. If teachers and administrators are to own the problem they must feel the problem personally or nothing much is likely to happen. How then, can we go about challenging faculties to get involved in producing significant reforms?

Getting Involved

Reformers, by definition, perceive a need to change. Change seems clearly desirable to them so it is easy to assume that, "any reasonable person can see that this is what we need to do". But people see things differently and views about what is necessary or desirable vary greatly from top to bottom of the school organization. Wonderful ideas, concocted by school boards, legislators or administrators may seem far less attractive to those who must put them to work. Teachers on the front line have their own needs and agendas to worry about. Hence, demands from upper levels of the professional ladder can easily be shrugged off as "just another nuisance" imposed by people, "who really don't know what the problems are". On the other hand, when originators up the administrative ladder observe this kind of foot dragging, it simply confirms what they thought in the first place; "teachers are apathetic, uninspired, unprofessional, self serving," or worse. So, top and bottom of the profession pass each other like ships in the night, and another attempt at reform bites the dust.

The process of continuing innovation is probably more important to a school system than the outcomes anticipated. To be engaged is the significant thing. Successful outcomes are happy events and help push the system toward greater effectiveness. More critical for the health of education and the self renewing schools we need is continued faculty participation, the encouragement of creativity and the experimental frame of mind. Even innovations which fail can contribute to growth; not only as lessons in what not to do, but for their contributions to broader understanding of the dynamics involved and the provision of leads to further exploration. The more we succeed in getting teachers and administrators involved in innovations the greater the likelihood for reform.

Clearly, the creation of a self renewing educational system will require new goals and understanding at every level; legislative, state and federal offices of education, school boards and administrators as well as in the front line work place. Nevertheless, if any change is to be successful, it must somehow enlist the cooperation of teachers and administrators responsible for translating the reform into action. To bring person-centered alternative schools into being at the work place level involves at least five important stages:

1. Creating challenge and expectations
2. Finding appropriate problems
3. Expanding awareness
4. Formulating strategies
5. Eliminating barriers

1. Creating Challenge and Expectations

First step in encouraging innovation is the creation of an atmosphere in which it can flourish. This calls for a widespread attitude in the workplace that it is good to look and fun to try, that change, experiment and innovation is the name of the game and mistakes are to be expected in the process. Skillful educational leaders are required to bring such an innovative esprit de corps into being. Unhappily, such attitudes clash with the need "to take no chances" or "play it safe" characteristic of most bureaucracies. Creating self renewal atmospheres requires constant effort to counteract the forces of tradition and inertia on one hand and to encourage exploration and risk taking on the other.

Feeling Adequate For Change

Earlier we defined challenge as the confrontation of events that interest the person and which he/she feels adequate to handle. Confronting important problems is thus only half the requirement for challenge. To feel challenged requires feeling reasonably able to cope. To meet that criterion, reform efforts must be concerned with how teachers see themselves. The experience of challenge is, in part, a function of positive or negative feelings about self, in part, a function of the size and difficulty of problems confronted and of teacher expectations. Research shows that good teachers see themselves in positive ways, as liked, wanted, acceptable, able persons of dignity and integrity. Poor ones do not. Whatever contributes to positive self concepts, therefore, gives teachers greater feelings of security and makes it more likely that problems of reform will be seen as challenges rather than threats.

Bolstering Self Esteem

Teachers and administrators who feel good about themselves are able to tackle new things with greater willingness and likelihood of success. When you feel sure of your self you can afford to take risks. Insecure people must play it safe and so resist taking chances. It follows that persons responsible for reform efforts must be aware of people's feelings about themselves and must do what they can to bolster self esteem. Psychologists and counselors call such awareness empathy: the ability to see things from the other person's point of view. It is a critical skill for teachers, counselors, social workers, administrators, indeed for anyone seeking to affect the behavior of other people. Recent researches on good and poor teachers reveal that a primary characteristic of good practitioners is an empathic attitude. Good teachers and administrators are constantly tuned in to how things look to the persons they are working with. They use that information to guide their decisions and behavior. Poor practitioners, on the other hand, are preoccupied with how things seem to themselves.

The capacity to be empathic is not a rare esoteric art. Quite the contrary. It is a skill we all learned in childhood. Children learn very early to be sensitive to how the grown ups around them are thinking and feeling. They have to. It is a matter of survival. Even a very young child may be heard saying to his sister, "Watch out for Mamma. She ain't feeling good". In the course of growing up each of us discovers that people around us behave according to their feelings and beliefs. Accordingly, we develop a keen sensitivity to how the important people in our lives are thinking and feeling and we adapt our own behavior in light of that knowledge.

This capacity for being sensitive to the feelings and attitudes of people around us continues throughout our lives. Unfortunately, it often becomes constricted in the process of growing up. As adults we are all highly sensitive to those who are important to us, lovers, husbands, wives, bosses, friends or enemies. With such persons we use our capacity for empathy well and often. Folks below us in the pecking order are another matter. We can afford to ignore the feelings and attitudes of children, employees, strangers, or social misfits, so we by pass the use of empathy. To be empathic as an educator does not require that we learn a new skill; only that we purposefully, systematically and in broader perspective do what we already know how to do with those who are important to us.

Beginning from awareness of how teachers are feeling about themselves, it is a simple step to determine what needs to be done to improve self esteem. As we have noted elsewhere one needs but to ask, "How can I help Ms. or Mr. X feel more liked, wanted, acceptable, able, dignified, worthy or professional?" Out of the replies to such questions will come suggestions for what is needed to create more positive self concepts in those we work with.

Professional Expectations

How people relate to problems is also dependent upon their personal expectations. People tend to live up to what is expected of them. "A" students are more likely to be achievers than "D" students. Teachers labeled as "goof offs" are likely to oblige. Administrators treated as "agents of the boss" tend to flex their muscles like he/she does. The things that seem important to teachers and administrators depend upon their professional expectations. They confront the problems they feel they should in local and traditional ways. It is a serious matter then, when teachers are treated as "delivery systems" or "cogs in the wheel". With such expectations it should not surprise us if they act so. Teachers without pride in their profession are unlikely to be much interested in reform.

In a profession like medicine where income is directly dependent upon performance and where medical discoveries and practices are newsworthy subjects for the media, doctors are strongly motivated to keep up to date. Advances in education, however, are seldom dramatic, life and death matters, or as concrete as a new machine or prescription. There are no right methods in teaching or administering. Instead, educational advances come about from the discovery or incorporation of ideas into practitioner's beliefs. Consequently they lack the drama and the specificity of a new drug, cat scan or operative technique. We also ply our profession, for the most part, out of the public eye, protected by the anonymity of a bureaucracy. In education, if you do your job reasonably well, no one asks more of you. In such a setting there is little motivation to keep abreast of the latest thinking or to risk the pitfalls of experiment and innovation.

If educators are to act as competent professionals, we will need to treat them as though they were. Effective reform requires a profession proud of itself and its mission. A demoralized profession cannot be counted upon to make the necessary changes. We need educators who see themselves as creative problem solvers in a dynamic, self-renewing profession. Such expectations for themselves must be endorsed and corroborated by public attitudes toward the profession. Teachers and administrators must act as entrepreneurs, addressing problems, inventing solutions and implementing ideas. To achieve such personal expectations they have to be treated as valued professionals, a requirement too often violated by administrators, legislators, school boards and parents to whom they are responsible.

Action Research

In the late forties and early fifties there existed an exciting movement in American education known as action research. The idea was that every teacher or administrator should be an active researcher in his/her own setting. Each practitioner would tackle some significant problem and experiment with promising solutions. For a time whole school systems began to get involved. Unhappily, the movement was brought to a halt with the launching of Sputnik. Citizens everywhere were horrified at this dramatic evidence that the Russians had beaten us into space. Searching for explanations, they blamed the schools for failure to produce the scientists we needed. To remedy matters, billions of dollars were poured into educational research and the production of research specialists. One unhappy result of this effort was to convince teachers everywhere that research was an esoteric activity that could only be performed by persons with advanced degrees in statistics and research design. The belief continues throughout the profession and seriously inhibits innovation and the processes of reform. We need a rebirth of the action research idea, a widespread movement that will encourage teachers and administrators at all levels to engage in the search for better ways to serve the youth in our schools.

A renewal of the action research movement is sorely needed. An effective program of reform requires that each teacher and administrator be actively engaged in trying something new at all times. Such an expectation ought to be an integral part of educational contracts. Many states require periodic updating of credentials through university credit or in-service training. We need to extend this expectation. One way might be to require personal exploration and discovery plans as regular requirements of employment. As part of his/her contract agreement each educator might file a plan for some innovation to be carried out during the year. Teachers of similar persuasion could file a group proposal or engagement of a faculty in one or more innovations might be a regular part of each year's agenda. People tend to live up to what is expected of them. It is time we treated teachers and administrators as creative, responsible professionals committed to continuous improvement of the system.

2. Finding Appropriate Problems

Front Line Problems

Since people are best motivated by personal need, the most promising route to reform is to begin from the problems that seem important at the front line. This proposal will probably seem frustrating to good hearted reformers. Front line problems often seem petty or unrelated to the "grand design" strategies conceived by upper level administrators and "experts". Watching teachers solve problems unrelated to the grand design seems like a reprehensible waste of valuable time and energy. It is not. Immediate personal needs take precedence over remote or foreign ones. That is a fact of life. We are more likely to make progress by accepting it than acting as though it did not exist. Major reforms will not come quickly. The task is too big and the numbers of people involved are too great for that. Better that faculties should work hard on problems to which they are committed than kill off promising reforms by half hearted participation.

The front line problems of teachers are not antagonistic to larger goals. Immediate questions like: How can I teach reading, math or geography? How can I help students be more responsible? How can I deal more effectively with discipline problems? How can I best prepare students for work or college entrance? are important problems for schools and teachers. Solving such problems will contribute to more person-centered schools as well. Because person-centeredness is not a method but a frame of reference for dealing with events, any local problem can be confronted within its scope. The questions just raised, for example, can result in significant progress toward person-centered goals. Person-centered approaches to reading, mathematics or geography will improve achievement in those subjects. Similarly, person-centered planning and treatment of students will result in greater responsibility and fewer discipline problems. Likewise, improved achievement and concern for student goals will improve preparation for work or college. It is not necessary to give up the goals of traditional schools to operate from person- centered assumptions. The application of person-centered thinking will help solve front line problems and simultaneously begin to move the system toward the kinds of schools required for modern reform.

Personal problems will always have first priority. Instead of ignoring or overriding them, helping to solve them will be more advantageous. Besides, the satisfaction of immediate needs makes possible the consideration of those on higher, broader levels. Teachers who are desperately trying to keep their heads above water with a difficult batch of students, using methods that do not motivate or trying to meet unrealistic curriculum goals are in no position to look favorably upon demands for reform, no matter how attractive or desirable they may be. The successful confrontation of current personal problems opens the way for consideration of those at other levels.

Discovering Needs

Two commonly employed strategies for discovering needs are the use of questionnaires and "needs assessment". It would seem logical simply to ask a faculty what its needs are. One way to do this is to make up a questionnaire and ask folks to check off the needs that seem most pressing to them. The findings are then assumed to represent vital needs of the faculty.

A second strategy for discovering needs is called "needs assessment". A school or faculty is encouraged to brain storm everything they can think of that their school or department needs in order to do its job well. Next, these needs are listed and prioritized by the group to reduce the items to a few of the most pressing or important ones. The resulting list is then accepted as goals for the reform effort and the group turns to finding ways to implement them in practice. Needs assessments and questionnaires seem like logical, business-like ways to investigate the needs of a faculty or school. One would think the procedures would be highly effective. As a matter of fact they often prove to be deeply disappointing.

Both procedures assume that one can get an accurate picture of people's needs by simply asking them, As a matter of fact there are dozens of reasons why the needs revealed in such procedures lead to disappointing outcomes. A major difficulty is that they do not really sample personal needs. Questionnaires which ask respondents to check needs from a list are restricted to those believed important by the test maker but may or may not have meaning for the participant. Similarly, needs assessments sample what people are ready, willing or can be seduced into saying are their needs. Such a sample may be a long way from the real needs motivating a faculty. We have seen that personal needs have priority over external ones. Mere public agreement that a need exists is no guarantee that it will ever be acted upon. Research on good and poor teachers has revealed that both good ones and bad ones make about the same scores on tests of professional matters. Both groups know what they ought to think and do. Only the good ones put their knowledge to work. When faculties have arrived at a consensus about their professional needs, they continue to behave in terms of their personal ones. Reform efforts must still face the problem of how to get professional needs transformed into personal ones.

Finding Hypotheses

A great many fine opportunities for innovation slip down the drain for lack of someone to hear problems stated and convert them into action. We have suggested the best source of innovations lies in local problems. These are constantly being confronted by teachers and spoken of in faculty meetings, conversation in the teacher's lounge, over lunch, etc. etc. Mostly they are aired and dropped without action. They can be turned into useful hypotheses for innovation, however, if someone is there to raise the question,

"What do you think is causing the problem?", "What do you suppose we could do about that?" or suggest, "Maybe that is something we ought to tackle together".

Other sources of hypotheses can be found in the reports of persons returning from professional conferences. People who attend such affairs are often intrigued by something that was said or happened there. Only rarely are such ideas carried into action because there is no follow up when the person returns to home base. Teachers and administrators who attend professional meetings should be invited to share what they learned. Whatever shows signs of exciting the reporter or the audience can then be followed up with questions like those in the paragraph above. Similar follow ups can be made after the visits of consultants, inspirational speakers or follow up of pertinent articles in professional journals.

A technique used by inventors can be equally profitable when used by reformers in search of innovative ideas. Beginning with the proposition, everyone washes dishes---no one should wash dishes, one investigator compiled several hundred alternatives. With a little imagination, the technique can easily be used by persons or faculties seeking educational matters to explore. One begins by asserting some generally accepted idea or practice, like, "grades are essential to student learning", "Competition is good for kids", "Students won't learn unless you make them" or, "There always have to be winners and losers in any situation". Next, one denies the assertion; "Students should not be graded" or, "It is not necessary that some must win and some lose". Now we are confronted with a problem to brain storm; what shall we do with this new assumption?" In the list of alternatives created there are sure to be several worth while hypotheses for innovation.

Hypotheses From The Literature

Educational literature is replete with promising hypotheses for exploration. Two publications from the Association for Supervision and Curriculum Development, for example, provide dozens of hypotheses derived from modern research and thinking. They are, <u>Perceiving, Behaving, Becoming: A New Focus For Education</u> (1962) and <u>Humanistic Education: Objectives and Assessment</u> (1978). The first is the association's 1962 yearbook. The second is a monograph report of the association's Working Group on Humanistic Education. Either of these publications is filled with forward looking ideas that can be effectively utilized as hypotheses for innovative efforts.

Here, for example, are six goals for educational reform taken from the Humanistic Education publication above (page 9 and 10):

"Goal 1. Education accepts the learner's needs and purposes and develops experiences and programs around the unique potentials of the learner.

Goal 2. Education facilitates self-actualization and strives to develop in all persons a sense of personal adequacy.

Goal 3. Education fosters acquisition of basic skills necessary for living in a multicultured society including academic, personal, interpersonal, communicative and economic survival proficiencies.

Goal 4. Education personalizes educational decisions and practices. To this end it includes students in the processes of their own education via democratic involvement in all levels of implementation.

Goal 5. Education recognizes the primacy of human feelings and utilizes personal values and perceptions as integral factors in educational processes.

Goal 6. Education strives to develop learning environments which are perceived by all involved as challenging, understanding, supportive, exciting and free from threat.

Goal 7. Education develops in learners genuine concern for the worth of others and skill in conflict resolution."

Each of these goals can be further delineated into more specific objectives suitable for experimentation or innovation.

Here is another list of "14 signs of creative teaching and learning" suggested in Perceiving, Behaving, Becoming (1962, p237):

"Less teacher domination; more faith that children can find answers satisfying to themselves.

Less teacher talk; more listening to children, allowing them to use teacher and the group as a sounding board when ideas are explored.

Less questioning for the right answer: more open ended questions with room for difference and the exploration of many answers.

Less destructive criticism: more teacher help which directs the child's attention to his or her own feelings for clarification and understanding.

Less emphasis on failure: more acceptance of mistakes--more feeling on the part of the child that when he or she makes a mistake it is done, accepted and that's it. As one child said, "She doesn't rub salt in".

Children's work is appreciated, but praise is not used to put words in the mouths of children.

Goals are clearly defined; structure is understood and accepted by the group.

Within appropriate limits, children are given responsibility and freedom to work. "For once teacher told us we could do it ourselves and really meant it."

Children are free to express what they feel and seem secure in their knowledge that the teacher likes them as they are.

Ideas are explored; there is an honest respect for solid information, an attitude of "let's find out".

There is a balance of common tasks and individual responsibility for specific tasks which are unique and not shared.

The teacher communicates clearly to children that learning is self-learning. Faith is demonstrated that all children want to become and pupils show satisfaction as they become aware of their growth.

Evaluation is a shared process and includes more than academic achievement.

Motivation is high and seems inner directed; pupil activity seems to say, "I've got a job I want to do".

Examples of how these goals can be established as objectives and effectively assessed may be found in Humanistic Education: Objectives and Assessment cited above.

These samples are merely illustrative. Many more objectives could be formulated by a faculty interested in finding ways to implement them with respect to any of the "goals" or "signs" listed above. Home grown objectives will also be more adaptable to local interests and conditions. While the literature is full of potential ideas for exploration, they are unlikely to be effective without local discussion and revision to suit the needs and interests of the faculty planning to put them to work.

3. Expanding Awareness

Choosing Problems To Be Addressed

We have made the point that many failures at reform are a consequence of laid on solutions, reforms generated from the top down. These seldom work effectively because they represent problems someone believes teachers should have rather than problems they do have. We have also seen that behavior is a direct function of human need and personal beliefs. Accordingly, we have advocated seeking reform from the bottom up, beginning with the problems teachers have. Tackling front line problems rather than "grand design" ones, however, runs the risk of never getting beyond the confines of crisis management. Simply responding to crises is responding to symptoms while fundamental causes remain in place and continue to thwart reform efforts. Counselors and psychotherapists know that the "presenting problem" is rarely the real issue. A similar observation could be made about reform. Immediate problems are only symptoms; if we never get beyond them, reform is unlikely. Some examples; concentration upon raising standards without improving teaching means more children will fail; providing tutoring for the ninth grade drop out overlooks earlier failures of motivation or helping students learn efficient study habits; dealing with discipline problems by making more rules only creates more rules to be broken. Though we begin with front line problems because teachers and administrators recognize and own them, they are not yet ready for innovation without a further step.

How can we utilize the motivating force of immediate personal problems to confront more fundamental or larger concerns? The answer lies in changing the focus of attention from crisis reaction to exploration and discovery of causes. The process begins by recognizing and accepting the validity of the problem for those confronting it, then taking the time to search for better understanding. Searching for solutions without examining the assumptions from which one begins ends in closed system thinking and endless variations on the same theme. Assuming change can be brought about by methods, fiat, or manipulation of things without reference to the belief systems of those involved in the process will keep reformers forever doing business at the old stand. Time spent exploring assumptions is not wasted. It provides the bed rock upon which belief and innovation can be built. Once a problem is confronted, therefore, the next step is to examine basic assumptions and related information. Let us take the drop out problem as an example:

If we ask why students drop out, we can get information from a wide variety of sources; from the literature and research, interviews with drop outs and their parents, examination of school records, information from school counselors etc., etc. Out of this information, it will be possible to build a list of hypotheses for further exploration. Such a list might include items like:

Student feelings of failure, rejection, embarrassment, alienation, helplessness, fear or anxiety.

Curricula which fail to challenge, which seem irrelevant to student needs or are beyond student capacity.

Seduction of the world of work, owning a car or dating attractions.

Failure of teacher-student relationships, resistance to restraint, unfair or high handed treatment or feeling no sense of control over one's own destiny.

Such expanded awareness about the presenting problem does two things: 1. it shifts the focus from simplistic manipulation of forces which are likely to be palliative, temporary or outright failures, and 2. it focuses attention on causes rather than symptoms and so leads to person-centered explorations with greater potential for lasting reform. This is the study and understanding phase of reform. When done well, it often suggests its own innovations. If you know that a drop out feels lost, you can institute ways to find him. If she is unchallenged by the curriculum, you devise a curriculum that challenges. If the school feels like a prison, you find ways to make it more user friendly, etc. 108

"It Takes Too Long"

At first glance beginning from local problems, then taking the time to expand awareness may seem like an unwarranted waste of time. Most failures at reform are a consequence of blind application of the manipulation of forces approach to solving problems. They are essentially reactive. They concentrate on <u>doing</u> something without reference to the belief systems of the persons involved. So, misbehavior is met with further restraint despite the fact that rebellion probably arose from restraint in the first place. Or, lack of achievement is met by raising standards instead of improving teaching. Or, the reluctance of teachers to comply with some annoying detail is made more annoying by demands for a written report. Reactive strategies lead to simplistic solutions without respect to causes.

Despite the fact that most educators are aware that first reactions don't get to the heart of matters, many continue to behave in reactive fashion because, they claim, "I don't have time to consider the problem more deeply". On a remote island in the Pacific, it is said, the natives have a belief that the worst thing that can happen to a person is, that his spirit may escape from his body. Accordingly, when a native gets sick, the family calls the medicine man and gathers around the patient to pray. If the patient continues to decline, they make a mixture of grass, mud and leaves and stop up all the patient's body openings. Under this treatment the patient always dies. But everyone feels better because they did something about it! Reaction solutions to educational problems are like that. Fundamental solutions or reforms take time and careful consideration of assumptions or causes. There is no quick or easy way. Many a promising innovation has been destroyed because its perpetrators were in too much of a hurry. Significant reform will not come about quickly. Generally speaking, the more important the reform effort, the more time it is apt to take to get it working. Research has shown that it is easy to go from democratic (open system) to autocratic (closed system) ways of dealing with people. It takes much longer to go the other way, from autocratic to democratic or from closed to open system thinking. Closed systems can easily be imposed, open ones require acceptance and cooperation of the participants. Effective experimentation requires patience. Adequate appreciation of time considerations can avoid much frustration when things get under way. Time is particularly important during the planning phases of an innovation when participants are beginning to grope toward common beliefs about the problem to be addressed and how to go about it. This means that meeting times should be flexible enough to pursue an idea to its conclusion without being cut off by time constraints.

"Suppose They Make The wrong Choice?"

A second objection is that, even if we take time to seek for causes; what guarantee do we have that people will choose the kind of answers required for reform? There is, of course, no absolute guarantee. Whenever you give people choice there is always the possibility that they will make some that you don't like. The risk is worth running, however, because reactive solutions are rarely more than palliative. Person-centered concepts are the result of fundamental research and experience. As a consequence they are less likely to fail than reactive solutions made from less accurate assumptions. Any reform effort, "worth its salt" must expect to make some poor choices from time to time. Being afraid to make mistakes is a sure way to discourage experimentation and creativity. Besides, intelligent persons, operating from the same assumptions and given real freedom for exploration, will probably arrive at similar. if not identical, conclusions anyhow.

4. Formulating Strategies

Strategy Preoccupation

A major cause of reform failure is the adoption of techniques or strategies without reference to basic assumptions or the readiness and capacity of teachers to carry them out. Much of the fix that current education finds itself in can be traced to its preoccupation with methods and things. The list of disappointing things oriented reform efforts in the first pages of this book are excellent examples. They are methods assumed to be right for general application to the system. They are a natural consequence of the seldom questioned manipulation of forces orientation characteristic of the system. If the behavior of teachers and students is a direct function of the forces exerted upon them, it follows that the way to influence their behavior is to manage the forces exerted upon them. As a consequence, from top to bottom the system is preoccupied with methods. The first questions typically asked by teachers and administrators when considering a problem are: "How can I----?", "What should I----?", "How do you---?", "What does he/she/they do----?". Meanwhile, far more important questions, having to do with basic assumptions, beliefs about goals, interrelationships and the nature of student learning and growth get comparatively little attention.

Many of education's problems never get solved because methods are applied to the obvious problem rather than the real one. Behavior, it must be understood, is only symptom. Strategies solely directed at managing behavior are palliative at best and can be highly destructive. For example, take the case of a typical delinquent who has learned over fourteen or fifteen years that "nobody likes me, nobody cares about me, everyone thinks I am no good". Feeling so, he comes to the conclusion, "Well, I don't like nobody neither!" and behaves in line with his/her conclusion by defiance and disruptive behavior (acting out, the psychologists call it). Such behavior, of course, is annoying, disruptive and unacceptable to teachers and administrators. In turn, they seek to control such obstreperous acts by techniques of management ---- punishment, ridicule, expulsion, embarrassment, failure, denial of privileges, law and order techniques, etc. etc. All these simply prove what the delinquent already believes-- "Nobody likes me. Nobody cares. Everyone is against me!".

Relating Strategy To Causation

Truly effective strategies must be related to <u>causes</u> rather than surface manifestations. First step in the selection of strategies, therefore, must be clear understanding of the dynamics involved as suggested in the Expanding Awareness section above. Even after appropriate strategies have been decided upon, the problem of side effects must be considered. Strategies are not worth much if they result in making matters worse. Even the most carefully plotted strategies can be accompanied by unforeseen concommitants. An elementary faculty decided to try to improve deportment by presenting a banner each week to the class with the best behavior record. They were totally unprepared for the result. Deportment got better in grades one through three but blew wide open in grades four to six. The younger children thought it an honor to get the banner while the older ones thought it a disgrace! Example: A certain high school granted the students' request for a student government. When the students came up with their first "law" teachers were horrified and vetoed the measure. The students returned to their task and soon came up with another which the teachers also vetoed. From this, the students got the message, "Our student government is only a game". So, they began to treat it as a game. This natural reaction was met by the teachers with exasperation and disapproval. "Why, they don't even treat their own student government as though it was serious", they complained, never grasping the fact that it was their own behavior that brought the unhappy consequence into being. Strategies with side effects that make things worse are no bargain.

We have seen that there are no universally right methods in education, that techniques or strategies are complex activities which have to fit a multitude of conditions. The principle holds for reform efforts as well. Reform strategies must fit the immediate problems, students, teachers, curricula and local conditions. We have also argued that good teachers must be entrepreneurs, skilled at confronting issues and finding or inventing appropriate solutions for them. Just so, the most promising source for effective reform strategies are those adopted or created by persons confronting the problems first hand.

No strategy, of whatever sort, is worth much if the user cannot employ it successfully. Methods must fit the practitioner. Accordingly, the preferred source of reform strategies should be those chosen or invented by teachers and administrators immediately responsible for face to face grass roots efforts. These have the additional advantage of being owned by the user with a consequent personal stake in its success. Even a personally devised strategy that fails can have salutary consequences in forcing the user to give up a dead end route of exploration to search for new avenues with greater promise.

Adopting Strategies

This is not to imply that the experiences or strategies invented or suggested by others are not useful. Other people's experience can, of course, provide helpful suggestions for strategy providing they are adapted to the local user and circumstances. The methods of other schools, teachers and administrators, however, can only serve as shopping lists or cafeteria displays from which innovators can choose techniques. They will need to be modified or adapted to local conditions and the new users. Many a promising strategy has failed because it did not fit the user and therefore was applied so tentatively or unskillfully as to defeat itself. This happens so often that it is probably a mistake ever to apply someone else's method without careful consideration of how it may be adapted to local conditions and personnel.

Suggestions for possible strategies lie everywhere. Traditional education has been so preoccupied with methods for so many years that the stockpile of strategies to choose from is enormous. Any teacher or administrator can name them by the dozens and the literature abounds with strategies that have worked successfully for some teacher or organization somewhere. Interested readers may find suggestions from which to begin explorations in many of the references to be found at the end of each chapter in this volume.

5. Eliminating Barriers

There are enormous barriers to innovation everywhere in the public school system. Some exist in philosophy, some in administration, some in practices that have become sacrosanct over the years, some in the curriculum, some in students and some in teachers or administrators themselves. One needs but to suggest an innovation and all sorts of objections come to light:

"There's nothing new about that. We've been doing that for years".
"It's only a fad. It will pass".
"I don't have time".
"You'll foul up our computers".
"They won't let you".
"We don't have a budget for that".
"It will never work".

Persons hoping to innovate, need to be prepared for such objections. I have been innovating all my professional life and one of the things I have learned is this; if you want to innovate, don't ask permission. Just do it and avoid publicity. Avoiding publicity makes it less necessary to deal with objections. In any life situation there is always room to wriggle. Even the most rigid circumstances leave some room for maneuver. By taking full advantage of such wriggle room, after a while people accept your position and give you more room to maneuver. If one takes up the slack continuously and in the same direction, it is possible to move a long way in a new direction before people become aware that you are deviating from standard procedure. When one day they discover you have left the traditional path, their objections are too late, providing you have kept records along the way and can show how well the innovation is working. At that point the conversation goes something like this:

Critic: "But you can't do that you know".

Innovator: "I can't ? Really? But look at the results I am getting".

Critic: "Well, that's good but according to the rules-----".

Innovator: "But I can't go back now".

Critic: "Well, we'll just have to find a way to make it legal".

Three very important barriers to innovation exist in the belief systems of teachers and administrators. These are:

The deeply held belief that there are right methods of teaching or administering. This myth is deeply ingrained in the profession and is constantly buttressed by "experts" who advocate one or another method as "the way". The myth is further solidified by preoccupation of the professional literature with methods. Since the methods any educator uses are in response to the unique situations they confront and their personal systems of beliefs, the methods teachers and administrators employ are necessarily different from those of their colleagues. Believing that there really are right methods, leaves practitioners with the sneaking suspicion that the methods they employ will not be able to stand up under scrutiny. Add to this the fact that, when they try someone else's touted method it frequently fails (because methods have to fit the user). So, the teacher or administrator arrives at a feeling of inadequacy, of being "not enough" and resolves to stick with his/her comfortable method rather than chance the confusion accompanying new ones.

To combat the sense of futility fostered by this belief we need to implement broad recognition:

1. Of the personal character of methods.

2. Of the significance of "fit" as the crucial determinant of methods.

102

3. That good teaching or administering does not require specific methods but the discovery of one's personal armamentarium of techniques.

These findings from modern theory and research deserve widest possible dissemination in the profession.

 The belief that innovation, research and experimentation requires high level skills in research design, statistics or assessment techniques. As a matter of fact, preoccupation with such skills can seriously interfere with front line innovation. Innovations ought to grow out of the teacher or administrator's local problems at the school or classroom level. Research and statistical experts rarely have the experience to understand or appreciate problems at such levels. Their competence lies with larger perspectives which frequently blind them to the significance of local problems. They speak a different language and have different goals from front line innovators. Too often their entrance into the picture results in distorting local problems to fit the research techniques in which they specialize. This twists the teacher's or administrator's problem into a shape they did not intend and which they feel incompetent to handle and corroborates the belief that they are inadequate to do research or innovate. Front line workers need to be disabused of these unfortunate beliefs. Instead, they need to be encouraged and rewarded for innovations around problems that concern them.

Valuable innovations need not meet high level standards of research design or statistical analysis. Being involved in the process of confronting problems and experimenting with solutions is, itself, a valuable experience. Significant information can be obtained at the grass roots level and important new practices can be invented or refined with the simplest of procedures, even with none at all. Experimenting with ways to help students feel better about themselves, learn to be more responsible or read more efficiently require little more than a teacher's good will and careful observation.

 The belief that mistakes are indicators of personal failure is another widespread roadblock to innovation. As we have seen, the entire educational system is built upon right answers. Mistakes or errors are regarded as reprehensible, if not condemnatory. But mistakes are inevitable in experimentation. They come with the territory. They must be expected, not feared. There is no such thing as a good or right way to teach and teachers must be seen as unique individuals. Good teachers do not have to be like anyone else. Errors and mistakes must be seen as acceptable concommitants of the innovative process. Even more, they must be regarded as valuable and useful to the self renewal effort, experiences from which to learn and improve upon thinking and practice.

Innovations are bound to be accompanied by difficulties of one sort or another. Panic reactions to these can have unfortunate long time effects unless innovators can learn to take them in stride. The scenario often goes like this: A teacher plans an innovation and begins to put it into operation. Students are surprised by this departure from "the way it"s sposed to be". They become uneasy and begin to test the limits of the new arrangement. This testing, in turn, raises the teacher's anxiety about whether the innovation will really work. The teacher's anxiety is communicated to the students who think, "Golly, our teacher isn't sure about what we are doing" and their anxiety level rises another notch. If now, something in the plan fails to work as expected, the teacher may throw in the towel, give up the innovation and go back to what is comfortable. So, a fine innovation may be lost because it never got carried out long enough to establish whether or not it was worthwhile. Worse still, thirty years later the teacher will still be maintaining, "That idea is for the birds. I tried it once and it doesn't work!". The real problem: the teacher was unable to give it a fair trial.

One way to avoid this unhappy scenario is to be sure that whatever innovation is attempted lies within the capacity of the persons to carry it out. Enthusiasm for a new idea can result in biting off indigestible sized projects and end in the kind of scenario illustrated above. Many innovations fail because the experimenter was not truly ready to tackle the problem. This is another reason why so many laid on reforms have failed in the past. Innovations need to be tackled in small bites, projects that can be comfortably handled by the practitioner within the circumstance and time frames available. Time spent in assessment of what can realistically be accomplished can save many heart aches and frustrated effort.

To escape the destructive effects of such myths as the three above, requires creating an atmosphere wherein they are systematically eliminated. The messages that there are no right methods, that anyone can innovate and mistakes are no big deal should be continuously fostered. Single efforts will not be enough. Myths die hard and the three above have been around for a long time. Combatting them will require continued effort to debunk them, on one hand, while advocating more positive alternatives, on the other.

A Search For The Barriers Strategy.

Early in my career I discovered a way of confronting barriers that has served me well on two fronts, suggesting innovations to try and clearing the road for smoother achievement of my goals. The strategy consists in asking the question, "What is keeping my students, (colleagues, co-workers) from------getting involved, asking questions, tackling problems----- whatever? I do this systematically in whatever setting I operate. Sometimes I ask my students, colleagues or employees directly. More often, I take the time to brainstorm the question at my leisure. The barriers I discover in this way are of all kinds. Some are in the circumstances, some in the curriculum, some in the methods I use, some in my colleagues, students and, all too often, in me. Once I have become aware of the barriers, I set about trying to eliminate them, one by one, as best I can. The strategy has paid big dividends. It has contributed much to my success as a teacher, administrator and researcher. It has also kept me continuously involved with exciting problems and, thus, spared me the pain and depression of professional burn out.

Some, barriers, of course, are in events outside my control, like the university catalogue, the registrar, budgets, equipment, space, school rules and regulations and the like. There is always a temptation to stop looking when those show up. They make it possible to avoid discomfort by shrugging problems off with a handy excuse, "Well, I could really do great things but THEY won't let me". I try not to succumb to such distractions and concentrate on the barriers I can do something about, especially those I discover in me.

Notes and References

References on good/poor teachers: See notes, Ch. 5.

References on self concept and self esteem: See notes,Ch.3.

General references:

Cincione-Coles, K. 1981. The future of education: Policy issues and challenges. Beverly Hills, Ca. Sage Publishers.

Combs, A. 1988. "New assumptions for educational reform". Educational Leadership,45,38-42.

Corbett,H. et. al. 1987. "Resistance to planned change and the sacred in school cultures". Educational Administration Quarterly, 33, 4, 36-39.

Sarason, S. 1982. The culture of the school and the problem of change, Boston, Allyn and Bacon.

On self esteem and empathy:

Georgiades, N. 1967. A study of attitudes of teachers to educational innovation. Doctoral dissertation, University of London.

Villars, J. 1989. "Schooling redesign: A key to educational restructuring". IN Hennes, J. Restructuring education: Strategic options required for excellence. Denver, Co. Colorado Department of Education.

On teacher expectations and action research:

Hopkins, D. 1985. A teacher's guide to classroom research Philadelphia, Pa. Open University.

Inman,V. 1984. "Certification of teachers lacking courses in education stirs battle in several states." Wall Street Journal January 6,39.

McKernan, C. 1988. "The countenance of curricular action research: Traditional, collaborative and critical- emancipatory conceptions". Journal of Curriculum and Supervision, Spring, 173-200.

Sanford, N. 1970. "What ever happened to action research?" Journal of Social Issues,26, 3-23.

Wallace, M. 1970. "A historical view of action research". Journal of Education for Teaching. 13,97-115.

Sources for innovative hypotheses:

ASCD, 1962. Perceiving, Behaving, Becoming: A new focus for education. Alexandria, Va. Yearbook, Association for Supervision and Curriculum Development.
118

ASCD, 1978. Humanistic education: Objectives and assessment. Alexandria, Va. Association for Supervision and Curriculum Development

Combs, A.W. 1982. A personal approach to teaching: Beliefs that make a difference Boston, Ma. Allyn and Bacon.

Combs, A. and Avila, D. 1985. Helping relationships: Basic concepts for the helping professions. Boston, MA. Allyn and Bacon.

Hamachek, D. 1970 The self in growth, teaching and learning. Englewood Cliffs, N.J. Prentice Hall.

Purkey, W. 1970. Self concept and school achievement. Englewood Cliffs, N.J. Prentice hall.

On innovative strategies:

Brandt, R. 1988 "On changing secondary schools: A conversation with Ted Sizer" Educational Leadership,46, 30-36.

Hall, G. and Hord, S. 1987. Change in schools: Facilitating the process Albany,NY, State University of New York Press.

Ornstein, A. 1982. "Change and innovation in curriculum". Journal of Research and Development in Education, 15,27-33.

CHAPTER 7

ALTERNATIVE SCHOOLS AND ASSESSMENT

We have made the point that every teacher or administrator ought to be involved in continuous experimentation as an expectation of the profession. But schools are communities and reform must be approached in groups as well as individually. Getting people involved in group innovations has many special advantages. We have seen in Chapter four that modern learning theory holds that feelings of identification or oneness are conducive to better learning. Working in groups expands and speeds the reform effort as more persons are involved in the process. More minds devoted to reform problems, means more opportunities to come up with good ideas and greater resources from which to draw solutions. Working in groups also has the advantage of providing mutual stimulation and discipline. A sense of loyalty to the group serves to reduce the shirking of responsibilities, bolsters determination in time of trouble and provides the support of shared jubilation in time of success. Furthermore, group unity supplies a common front against the criticism and outside pressures that, almost inevitably, accompany innovative efforts.

Organizing Groups For Reform

Most productive groups consist of like minded persons tackling a problem of common interest. Since communication and participation are essential, groups need to be small enough to give everyone opportunity to be known and heard. The optimum number is probably about 8 or 9 with the maximum about 14. In the beginning, group members must be interested in the problem and willing to commit themselves to the process. They need not be identically minded at the outset. Neither should they be so disparate as to make achieving agreement an impossible goal. Members of successful groups generally grow closer to one another fairly quickly in the course of participation but the process ought not be made more difficult than necessary. Most effective groups operate in the open system outlined in Chapter 4. Group members should be involved, not only in deciding what to do about a problem. They should also be deeply involved in the process of defining the problem at the outset and exploring its ramifications thereafter. Every effort should be expended to make group sessions as challenging and unthreatening as possible.

Much will depend upon the skill of the group leader. Helping a group design and carry out a significant reform effort is a demanding task. It requires depth of understanding about the dynamics of group interaction and the ability to facilitate discussion, protect and encourage participants, to sense group readiness or resistance and to help the group achieve its mission in the most salutary fashion. Every school system needs persons on the faculty who are possessed of such group process skills. Subsidizing group dynamics training of several faculty persons is a valuable investment for schools seriously concerned about reform. Hiring an outside facilitator is a second option but having good group facilitators already on board is an asset for any school.

The Need For Consensus

Group approaches to reform are dependent upon consensus. The success of any innovation is dependent upon persons with like or congruent belief systems. Gaining agreement by taking a vote is not enough. Calling for a vote is often no more than a device to stop discussion. When a majority feels sufficiently strong to carry a decision, it calls for a vote. Winning the vote is a satisfaction for the winner but leaves the loser feeling coerced into going along. It runs the risk of driving resistance underground and subverting the decision making process. Group members holding implicit or explicit antagonisms or hidden agendas are a drag on the innovative task. Consensus is time consuming and often frustrating but, in the long run, provides greater prognosis for success. Effective group innovations require like minded teachers or administrators. Much depends upon mutual respect, open communication and general agreement on fundamental assumptions and strategies. It is only when people are thinking and believing alike that consistent and compatible action can be counted on.

Effective innovations are dependent upon persons who, because of their similar convictions, can be counted upon to confront problems and find solutions congruent with the group's philosophy and intent. Such like mindedness takes time to develop. It comes about as a consequence of shared discussion and mutual experience and once established should be carefully nurtured. A common cause of failure with group innovations is brought about by the entrance of new members into a group after it is well under way. New members to a group disrupt existing patterns. Each new person introduced makes it necessary for the group to reorganize its relationships. Precious time must be spent bringing the new members up to speed. This can prove to be a frustrating, disruptive experience for all concerned. Nearly always it delays progress. It can also defeat the group's goals by destroying the consensus necessary to cooperative effort.

Why Innovations Disintegrate

It is a common occurrence that highly promising educational innovations disintegrate after a few years of successful operation. A major reason seems to lie in the insertion of new members to the group, withdrawal of original workers or attempts to institutionalize the reform. When founding members of the innovative group depart, the group loses an integral part of its process. This loss is compounded if departing members are replaced by individuals of different persuasion who have not shared in the evolution of the group's thinking and experience. The effect is even more devastating if the new entrants are antagonistic to the innovative effort or unwilling to adapt their belief systems to the group's goals and processes.

These dynamics also explain why innovations can rarely be institutionalized. Example: A truly significant innovative teacher preparation program was designed in the seventies by a group of twelve faculty members and placed in operation side by side with the more traditional existing program. The new program proved so successful that it attracted attention from foreign lands as well as here in the United States. Then, one day, after several successful years, the department voted to adopt the new program for all students and phase out the old one. This attempt to institutionalize the program did it in. Faculty members long accustomed to the thinking and practices of the traditional program found themselves thrown overnight into a very different philosophy and way of working. Despite the good intentions of the faculty who voted to adopt the program, the thinking, planning, and belief systems developed by the original group of innovators could not be quickly incorporated into the belief systems of those injected into the program. This created enormous anxiety for the new faculty and frustration for the founding members. Their insecurity was quickly conveyed to the students who were, themselves, adapting to a program quite different from their traditional college classes. Student anxiety, in turn, only corroborated the insecure feelings of the faculty. Inability of the new instructors to understand or cope with the program's innovative concepts and practices began a rapid disintegration. In spite of the department commitment, they began to pull back to more familiar and comfortable ways of thinking and teaching. The break up was hastened by the departure and replacement of several of the innovation's originators. Within two years this highly significant innovation was so eroded as to be almost indistinguishable from the traditional program it replaced.

The essence of an innovative program lies not in philosophy, equipment or techniques but in the belief systems of its proponents and practitioners. Without a common system of beliefs to give meaning and consistency to methods and information, innovations quickly disintegrate or self destruct though a cacophony of mixed messages. It is the quality and congruence of the beliefs held by the practitioners that supplies the glue to hold things together and the guidelines for staying on track.

The Need For Participant Protection

Deviations from common practice invite opposition. Innovations which depart very far from traditional modes of operation are practically certain to run into criticism. It takes courage, an adventurous spirit and a thick skin to try new things. Glitches are inevitable in any creative effort and are bound to be accompanied by fumbling efforts and trial and error learning in their early phases. Innovations also take time and salutary results may not be apparent until the experiment has run its course. A major responsibility for supervisors, therefore, must be to shield innovators from some of the most destructive criticism brought on by their departure from the status quo. To carry a program past such shoals to smoother sailing requires protective measures from the administration.

One device to reduce criticism and opposition is to label the new program "experimental". Much destructive criticism can be avoided if the school or system has a general atmosphere favoring experimentation. The term "experiment" sounds temporary and less threatening to observers. Calling an innovation "experimental" can often help suspend customary rules and regulations and protect an innovation long enough to get itself established. When innovation is the name of the game and everyone is participating, the likelihood of destructive criticism is greatly reduced. Even so, particular innovative efforts may be misunderstood and become the subject of attacks. To maintain morale and support for reform, administrators may need to come to the defense of persons engaged in worth while experiments.

Multiple Innovations

Too often, reform attempts are concentrated in a single effort, building or system. Ideally, a reform minded system will have everyone involved in some kind of innovation one way or another, either as individuals or as groups. This means that reform efforts of several kinds may be operating side by side. Simultaneous innovations have many advantages. With many people involved, the problem of dealing with criticism is greatly reduced and alternative choices are offered to unhappy participants. Multiple experiments also make comparisons among programs possible and speed the processes of reform. They have the advantage of increasing the options for consumers. Instead of a monolithic "take it or leave it" program, consumers are given choice of alternate ways to work and achieve their goals. The University of

Ottawa, for example, has three programs for teacher education which run simultaneously and students are permitted to choose the program that best suits their needs. The University of Northern Colorado Laboratory School is organized in "families" of fifty children with three congenial teachers. Each family is conducted by its teacher team in a fashion consistent with their beliefs, the curriculum and the needs of the particular students they are responsible for. Each family's pattern is also congruent with the school's overall mission which is, itself, innovative. An additional advantage of such side by side programming is the stimulus it provides for faculty discussion and the generation of new ideas or hypotheses.

Provision For Review

Major innovative efforts should be subject to a time limit and review process. Innovators need to be accountable. One way of achieving this is to legitimize innovations through contractual agreements in which participants agree upon a "contract" describing the project they propose, the hoped for outcomes and a proposed date for review and justification. When the justification date approaches, arrangements can be made for an audit of the program, preferably including some outside persons. Following the audit, decisions can be made to continue the project, revise it or phase it out. If the innovation is phased out participants are freed to file a new proposal or join an on-going program to which they can make a contribution.

In establishing a review process, care must be taken to avoid inhibiting the innovation by unnecessary paper work or the imposition of crippling restraints. Audit plans and criteria must be made with full participation of the innovative team. The intent of time limits and audits is not to control and direct the program. Instead, they are designed to assure participants sufficient time to test their hypotheses and a process for demonstrating outcomes, revising goals and practices or discontinuing the effort without prejudice.

Alternative Schools

We have advocated achieving reform by encouraging innovation among individual teachers and administrators as a professional expectation. We have also called for group innovations at the level of program development. The logical next step is alternative schools. We need diversity and innovation among schools as well as in classrooms and programs. Indeed, successful facilitation of innovations at individual and program levels must inevitably lead to a wide array of alternative schools. There is a rising tide of demand, both inside and outside the profession, for the break up of huge schools and the establishment of smaller ones. The national report, A

<u>Nation At Risk,</u> and the leadership of the National Education Association and the American Federation of Teachers have each called for alternative schools as a necessary step toward educational reform.

There is also a growing public demand for "schools of choice". However, there is so little diversity within the monolithic character of most existing public schools that present choice is limited to going public or private. To provide real choice for consumers and true self renewal for the system, we need far more diversity. A large number of alternative schools are called for, each based upon sound fundamental assumptions, implemented by like minded professionals and adapted to the peculiar needs of the students and communities they serve.

Alternative schools make sense in light of what we know about the diversity of students and how they learn. Educators have long recognized, intellectually, the importance of individual differences in students. They have also advocated, theoretically, that public schools adapt to such differences. In practice, however, our schools have spent far more energy seeking ways to ignore the fact of individual differences. We have sought to group students homogeneously by tracking, grade levels, psychological tests, or special classes for the handicapped or gifted. But the problem refuses to go away. As Earl Kelley once said, "We have these marvelous schools, rich curricula, excellent teachers. Then--Damn it all, the parents send us the wrong kids!"

More recently, we have learned from brain research and child development studies that students have different learning styles and failure to take cognizance of that fact can inhibit student progress or even shut down learning all together. Add to this what modern research tells us about good teaching: that there are no "right" methods, that good teachers operate from personal beliefs about themselves, their students and ways of going about their professional practice. Such findings call for diversity in learning and teaching at every level, with individuals, programs or alternative schools.

All these reasons for moving to alternative schools are difficult to implement in the face of current preoccupation with bigness, standardization, the industrial model and reliance upon the manipulation of forces approach to planning and action. We are immobilized by outdated thinking, the drive for interchangeable parts and an enormous investment in huge plants and facilities. In addition, the inertia of bureaucracies militates against innovation and diversity. Everywhere else in our society we applaud the findings of research and scramble to purchase and enjoy the fruits of experimentation converted into goods and services. That is the way we Americans have attained the high quality of our life style. We need now to apply the same attitudes toward modern thinking and research in education. It is time to reduce the widening gulf between the best we know and the ways we try to teach. Alternative schools are an important step in that direction. We have at our disposal an exciting array of new thinking, research and practice. It remains for us to find ways to put it to work.

Alternatives or Holding Tanks?

There are a growing number of alternative schools about the country. Too often they are planned and operated as "holding tanks" for potential drop outs or misfits within the system. In many districts they are shunted off to remote and inadequate quarters, staffed by indifferent personnel and treated as inferior, even embarrassing appendages to the system, much like we treat our prisons. A comparative few are designed around innovative philosophy or a like minded faculty. Even then, alternative schools are too often reserved for discipline cases or potential drop outs. Here and there one finds a fascinating institution open to all students and attempting to implement ideas from modern thinking or research and staffed by creative, enthusiastic teachers. Even where such schools exist they are too often regarded as mere ornaments, indicators that the system is in touch with the times or as sops to quiet the complaints of liberal minded parents.

I was once privileged to participate in the audit of three alternative schools in a large school system in Colorado. Our committee was deeply impressed with the programs, school climate, student achievement, adaptations to individual differences and the professionalism of staff. It was a delight to observe these schools in progress and to observe the interaction of students and teachers. Here were three schools, two person-centered and one highly structured"back to basics" program, each successfully and happily experimenting with a set of basic assumptions about what teaching and learning ought to be like. Several parents commented to us, "Why should schools like this be reserved for only a few? All kids ought to have this kind of school!". Entrance to these schools was on a "first come, first served" basis. Each had waiting lists with more applicants than their total populations. We reported, in part, to the school board, " We find these schools to be excellent, with programs far in advance of traditional schools. It is also clear from the length of their waiting lists, that there exists real demand for alternative schools in your community. We recommend the establishment of more such schools as soon as practicable to meet those demands". The recommendation was graciously accepted and generally ignored.

Starting Alternative Schools

A prime key to the success of alternative schools, like the success of any innovation, is a like minded faculty. A group of professionals fired with an idea they believe in can create an exciting and significant alternative school. Common beliefs and the freedom to explore and implement them hold innovations together. Widely disparate beliefs can quickly erode an alternative school, bring its progress to a halt and reduce the program to just another group of pedantic individuals each doing their thing without reference to each other or to an overall strategy. Starting an alternative school can be most effectively approached in either of two ways: 1. by encouraging teachers within the system to draw up proposals they would like to try, or, 2. formulating an idea to be implemented, then recruiting a committed staff to carry it out.

The first approach is most expeditious. It is always easier to begin from the beliefs people already have than to sell a set of new ones. Getting started is also facilitated if participants already know each other and have worked together on some group innovation in being. This provides opportunity to begin from an already tested hypothesis and a cadre of experienced persons around whom to organize. It has the further motivational value of rewarding a successful innovation by expansion, affirmation and publicity.

The second option is more difficult. It also runs the risks inherent in laid on solutions. One must first find a way to sell the idea. To do that requires building a common set of beliefs among the participants. This can be speeded up somewhat by recruiting persons intrigued by the basic hypothesis. Even with such a beginning, however, the process of discussion and achievement of consensus, can be a difficult and time consuming affair. There is a substantial difference between intellectual espousal of an idea and the discovery of its personal meaning at a level deep enough to find its way into action. Failure to recognize this distinction between intellectual knowing and personal belief has brought about the downfall of many a well intentioned reform. Taking the time and making the effort to achieve common meanings is not time wasted; it is an essential requirement for a successful alternative school.

Alternative schools require a maximum of on site control. Such independence is difficult to achieve in most school systems. Large bureaucracies do not take kindly to parts taking off on their own. Nor do management oriented administrators look with favor on relinquishing control of subordinate phases of the system. Surmounting such roadblocks requires a secure and forward looking administration. By definition, alternative schools must depart from tradition and standardization to confront new ideas and new ways of working. That calls for administrators who see themselves as facilitators, rather than managers, who are comfortable with open system thinking and secure enough within themselves to permit delegation of major responsibility to the faculties of alternative schools.

The Large Plant Problem

A major handicap to reform and the establishment of alternative schools lies in the existence of thousands of expensive buildings and grounds designed for large numbers of students. These hangovers from thirty or forty years of big school thinking have now become a hindrance to today's reform movement. With growing recognition of the need for diversity and alternative schools they stand like, "elephants in the living room", embarrassments that must somehow be circumvented. The investment in such plants is enormous and few communities are likely to countenance the abandonment of outmoded plants and facilities. As a consequence, the alternative schools movement will have to make use of and adapt to existing facilities in many, if not most, communities.

To fit alternative schools into existing plants, strategic planners have sometimes recommended an organization of "houses" within the building. Each "house" would represent an alternative school with its own autonomous faculty committed to a common set of beliefs and an appropriate student body. Each "house" would also operate as a separate entity with its students and faculty spending most of each day together, but free to leave the "house" as needed to utilize the resources of athletic, art, music, shop or other special facilities.

Optimal size for an alternative school will vary greatly from community to community. The most efficient size for such facilities will be dependent upon many factors including: faculty morale, the characteristics of the student body, curricula and school objectives, administrative and budgetary constraints, the freedom of operation and communication among faculty and the quality and skill of the school's leadership. Some reform minded planners have suggested 400 students as a maximum size for an efficient alternative school. Beyond this figure the capacity of an alternative school to achieve modern objectives becomes seriously impaired. With so many variables involved in the determination of size, it is clear that optimum figures must be determined locally.

Some Criteria For Designing Alternative Schools

It is not my purpose here to prescribe a pattern for alternative schools. I am convinced that it is only through their establishment in the widest possible diversity that the changes required to reform our educational system can be brought about. To be locally successful, however, and to contribute maximally to the national effort, alternative schools must represent a creative mix of three primary factors:

1. They must fit local needs, conditions and student bodies.

2. They must be designed to implement the best we know from modern theory and research.

3. They must be designed and operated on site with the greatest possible freedom of action for a like minded, committed professional staff.

How these factors are integrated in a particular setting will be determined by the nature of each school's faculty. Instead of the territorial restraints imposed by rigid job descriptions, faculties will work out functions and responsibilities as a team, utilizing the peculiar talents and skills of each member in the most effective ways possible. No outsider will be capable of designing an effective alternative school. Nor will it be possible to lift a successful plan from one community to another without modification. There are no universally right patterns. Alternative schools must fit local goals, students and faculties. As for ideas around which alternative schools may be organized; there are hundreds in the literature from which to choose and many more to be invented on the spot. Effective reform comes about through trying, experimenting with promising hypotheses by a like minded professional faculty. There is even room for failures and mistakes. Indeed, discovering that a particular innovation is defective or inadequate is, itself, a worthwhile contribution to the overall goal of reform. We will have more to say about the roles of alternative school teachers and administrators in the next two chapters but let us pause here for a consideration of how such programs and schools may be monitored.

Assessing Reform Efforts

One of the unhappy outcomes of preoccupation with the manipulation of forces and the industrial model has been a passion for objectivity and statistics in the evaluation of education. Unless an event can be measured and reported in numerical terms it tends to be discounted. As a consequence, evaluative efforts concentrate almost exclusively on academic achievement expressed as facts known, words spelled, problems solved or similar matters that lend themselves to counting and statistical manipulation. This preoccupation with objectivity restricts evaluation of educational outcomes to the acquisition of information or the performance of directly measurable skills. Because such matters can be handily counted and simply expressed, they become the exclusive criteria by which the effectiveness of the system is judged. Worse still, because the system is evaluated in numerical terms, reform efforts concentrate on countable processes. This restricts reforms to the simplest most obvious objectives while broader, more important goals are ignored altogether. Broader, more humane objectives like responsibility, interpersonal relationships, habits, attitudes, feelings, problem solving, beliefs, concern for others, values, aspirations and convictions never appear among assessments of the system. Instead, we fret about achievement test scores and strive to bring everyone above average as though that were possible. We are shocked to find students are unable to locate Afghanistan or Tanzania on a world map.

A major reason why reform is currently so necessary is that society is asking much more of its schools and the future is requiring much more of students. But many of these new demands do not lend themselves to simple observation or counting. How, for example, do you count a positive self concept, openness to experience, feelings of identification, responsibility, trustworthy values, adapting to change, learning how to learn or coping with violence and conflict ? How shall we assess an innovative program or an alternative school? Clearly, we shall have to go beyond counting and statistics.

Fundamental changes in objectives often make it necessary to devise new approaches to evaluation. This often requires working with imprecise forms of assessment until better ones can be invented. Accordingly, innovators must expect that early efforts at measurement may be cruder than they might like. The first experiments with atomic fission at the University of Chicago were also extremely crude but advanced our knowledge of atomic power. The Wright brothers first airplane was a far cry from the technological marvels of today's aircraft. Just so, the assessment of new objectives and ways of working are likely to be less precise than we might wish. That fact ought not deter us from utilizing new approaches to evaluation. It is not necessary to give up the use of customary objective devices entirely. We need to use them when they are appropriate. Beyond the objective, behavioral devices with which we are familiar, however, we may also need to employ one or more of the following to get at some of the personal, social and attitudinal goals important for educational reform.

The Use Of Inference

Modern objectives, like responsibility, concern for others, attitudes, values, beliefs and convictions do not lend themselves to behavioral measurement. Similarly, recent researches on good and poor teaching have demonstrated that the distinguishing criteria for good teachers lie, not in knowledge or methods, but in the teacher's belief system. Accordingly, if we wish to assess student growth or teacher characteristics in anything but the most superficial ways, we shall have to find ways of exploring student or teacher perceptions. But belief systems lie inside the person and so are not available to direct external assessment. They can, however, be sampled by inference. People behave in terms of their feelings, perceptions or beliefs. It follows, that if we observe their behavior carefully, we ought to be able to infer the nature of the perceptions which produced those behaviors. This is the process of empathy, seeing things from the point of view of whatever persons one is dealing with which we have alluded to in previous chapters.

Although everyone uses inference or empathy daily to interact with the important people in their lives, it is rarely employed in educational assessment. The profession has been preoccupied with objectivity and traditional tests and measurement devices for evaluation of students or the system itself. The use of inference is also widely regarded as unscientific and unacceptable. As a matter of fact, the technique is widely used in science to cope with events that cannot be directly observed. For example, astronomers pin point the location of stars no one has ever seen by inferring their location from other data. Though no one has ever seen electricity, we are able to infer its existence and behavior. Likewise, all of us predict what is going to happen tomorrow or further in the future from observations we make today.

Inference is especially useful for dealing with events that cannot be observed directly or for projecting the nature of events in the future. It is also a necessary technique for educators concerned with the assessment of such objectives as values, attitudes, self concept, teacher purposes, concern for others etc. Such matters do not lend themselves to objective evaluation.

The Use Of Judgement

A major goal of education is the improvement of human judgement. Though it is palpably open to error, it is often the only available source of data for assessment of some educational objectives. But human judgement is generally rejected as a source of evidence for the achievement of educational goals and objectives. It can, however, be subjected to disciplined use and so made more reliable. Judgements can, for example, be required to meet tests of internal or external reliability, capacity to predict, logic, experimentation and demonstration. Data obtained by making judgements are too valuable to be summarily rejected.

It is interesting to contrast public attitudes toward professional opinion in education with other professions like engineering, medicine or law. Professional opinion in those occupations is generally treated with respect and accepted as valid observations. People who would not think of questioning the recommendations of a physician, lawyer or engineer, feel free to make light of professional recommendations made by educators. This happens even within the profession. Lack of confidence in the opinions of educators may be due, in part, to the system's exclusive reliance upon objective approaches to testing and evaluation. Part also seems to be spawned by the demoralization of the profession and the widespread public assumption that "anyone can teach". Currently, there are even serious attempts to eliminate the professional aspects of teacher education altogether and to open the profession to anyone who can demonstrate competence in a subject matter area. The degradation of professional opinion is a serious handicap to reform. It undermines teacher/administrator confidence, discourages involvement in reform efforts and contributes substantially to guaranteeing their prompt demise. Ignoring professional opinion from those upon whom success depends eliminates critical input in the planning phases of reform and enormously increases the likelihood of failure.

Professional opinion growing out of years of experience must be respected. It can contribute much to the assessment of reforms. Professional opinion, like any other assessment device, is subject to limitation. It can, of course, be biased and unreliable but that fact hardly warrants its complete rejection. Professional judgement can be subjected to tests of reliability like any other measuring instrument. They can also be screened for prejudice, conflict of interest and other sources of distortion.

Objective data has little relevance until it is refined and interpreted by professional judgement. Some events can only be effectively assessed by reference to professional opinion and innovators ought not shy away from this valuable source of information. The human brain has enormous capacity to perceive, absorb, assimilate and interpret vast numbers of observations. Professional opinion is worthy of respect and should be included without apology as a vital factor in the planning, operation, revision and evaluation of reform efforts.

Critical Incidents

An often overlooked source of evaluative data are critical incidents, single events which reveal with special clarity the dynamics of a process. These can often tell a practiced observer much more than a book full of test results. The spontaneous outpouring of student affection and concern for an injured classmate or teacher, for example, tells reams about the relationships in that classroom. Likewise, the ways in which people speak about matters can often be highly revealing of their attitudes, values, beliefs, hopes fears, and prejudices. Psychologists call this "listening with the third ear" to the meanings that lie behind people's verbal or non verbal behavior. Because people behave according to their beliefs, it is possible to "read behavior backwards" to understand the beliefs that are motivating them. For example: Teachers who talk of "making" people do this or that are revealing their preferred strategy in student relations. Similarly, expressions of scorn, put downs or questions about people's capacities can tell an observer much about an administrator's management style.

Experiential Data

A most important way to obtain data with respect to people's attitudes and beliefs, of course, is to query the consumer. If you want to know what someone is thinking or feeling, you can ask them. That seems obvious enough and evaluators often attempt to gather data about what people think and feel by the use of questionnaires. Questionnaires have the additional advantage of converting data into numbers. This provides the illusion of objectivity and the comfort of familiarity because results can be treated in the same fashion as traditional tests and measurements. Unfortunately, what persons say they think, feel, value or believe may be a far cry from their actual perceptions. All sorts of factors get involved in determining the accuracy of a person's reply to the question, "What do you think about----?" Here are just a few determiners of the responses participants may make: Whether the responder:
 thinks it is any of the questioner's business,
 trusts the questioner,
 really has an opinion,
 feels an obligation to reply,
 has an agenda of his/her own to advance,
 knows what the questioner is seeking,
 has the language to express a reply,
 Etc., etc., etc.

Despite such sources of possible error, consulting consumers about their feelings, attitudes, beliefs and understandings is a necessary and desirable source of data for the assessment of reforms. Just as the physicist calibrates her instruments before taking measurements, so too, can the accuracy of personal reports be substantially increased by creating the most facilitative atmospheres for the persons responding. Generally speaking, experiential information is most likely to be accurate when responders feel: trust in the questioner, free of threat in the situation, certain there will be no adverse consequences for sharing, interested in the matter under discussion and assured that some personal; benefit will accrue from the exchange.

Notes And References

Alternative school directories:

National Association of Laboratory Schools, 1989. <u>Directory 1988-1989</u> 104 Davis Hall, Indiana University of Pennsylvania, Indiana, PA. 15705

The National Coalition of Alternative Community Schools. 1990. <u>1989-1990 National Directory of Alternative Schools</u>. 58 Schoolhouse Road, Summertown, TN, 38483.

General references:

Constans, P.1980. <u>Fit for freedom</u> Lanham, MD. University Press of America.

McDonald, J.1988. "The emergence of the teacher's voice: Implications for the new reform". <u>Teachers College Record</u> 89, 471-486.

Smith, J. 1987 <u>Educating teachers: Changing the nature of pedagogical knowledge</u> New York, Palmer Press.

Swartzbaugh, P. 1988 "Elementary teaching successfully". <u>Educational Leadership</u> 45, 20-24.

Facilitating change:

Little, J. 1989. "Assessing the prospects for teacher leadership" IN <u>Building a professional culture in schools</u> New York, Teachers College Press.

Maeroff,G. 1988. "A blueprint for empowering teachers" <u>Phi Delta Kappan</u> 69: 472-479.

Rogers, C. 1967. "The interpersonal relationship in the facilitation of learning" IN <u>Humanizing education: The person in the process</u> Alexandria, Va. Association for Supervision and Curriculum Development.

On restructuring schools:

Association for Supervision and Curriculum Development, 1988. "Restructured schools: Frequently invoked, rarely defined" <u>Update</u> Alexandria, Va. Association for Supervision and Curriculum Development.

Lieberman, A. 1988. Building a professional culture in schools. New York, Teachers College Press.

Mc Donald, G.1989. "When outsiders try to change schools from the inside". Phi Delta Kappan 71,206-211.

Raywid, M. 1984. "Synthesis of research on schools of choice" Educational Leadership April 1984, 71-78.

Raywid, M. 1987. "Public choice, Yes: Vouchers, No!" Phi Delta Kappan 87, 766.

On alternative schools:

Association for Supervision and Curriculum Development, Removing barriers to humaneness in the high school. Alexandria, Va. Association for Supervision and Curriculum Development.

Boyer, E. 1988. "A generational imperative: Educate all our children" The Generational Journal 1988, 1-5.

Clinchy, E. "Public school choice: Absolutely necessary but not sufficient" Phi Delta Kappan 71, 289-294.

Dade County Schools. 1988. School based management: Shared decision making. Miami, FL. Dade County Public Schools.

Glenn, C. 1989. "Putting school choice in place." Phi Delta Kappan 71, 295-300.

Gregory, T. 1986. "Alternative schools as Cinderella: What the reform reports didn't look at and don't say" Changing Schools 13,2-4 and 14, 2-5.

King, S. 1988. "Bronxville High: An "essential" school in process. Educational Leadership41, 35-38.

Nathan, J. 1989. "Helping all children, empowering all educators: Another view of school choice". Phi Delta Kappan 71, 304-307.

On assessment and accountability:

Association for Supervision and Curriculum Development. Humanistic education: Objectives and assessment. Alexandria, VA. Association for Supervision and Curriculum Development.

Combs, A. 1973. Educational accountability: Beyond behavioral objectives. Alexandria, Va. Association for Supervision and Curriculum Development.

Combs, A. et. al. 1969. Florida Studies in the helping professions. Gainesville, FL. University of Florida Press.

Fantini, M. 1977. "Toward a redefinition of American education". Educational Leadership 35, 167-172.

Wascicsko, M. 1978. The effect of training and perceptual orientation on the reliability of perceptual inferences for selecting effective teachers Doctoral dissertation, Gainesville, FL. University of Florida.

CHAPTER 8

REVITALIZING THE PROFESSION

No program of educational reform, however desirable, will meet with much success without the commitment and support of teachers. These are the front line workers upon whom the entire process depends. Traditionally, teaching has been regarded primarily as a how-to skill; the ability to inculcate students with a body of information and the techniques required to apply it. This conception has pervaded all aspects of our society. The public and its legislators think of teaching as a matter of being informed in subject matter and knowing how to deliver it. Administration's focus upon the industrial model is also predicated upon such a concept of teaching and the manipulation of forces approach to dealing with problems corroborates such a mechanistic view of the profession. The attitude is widely shared within the profession by many teachers and administrators resulting in a preoccupation with finding right methods to carry out their tasks. Administrators search for better ways to manage students and teachers while teachers keep searching for simpler, surer methods to get students to learn the prescribed curriculum. The "delivery system" concept is further perpetuated by pre- service and in-service teacher education.

A New Appreciation Of The Profession

Since people behave according to their beliefs, so limited a view of the education profession is a major hindrance to reform. To attain the self renewing, person-centered schools today's society sorely needs, a broader, more dynamic conception of the profession is required. Instead of regarding teachers as delivery systems or clever manipulators of subject matter and persons, we need understanding of the educator's task as a true profession. Teaching must be seen as a process of facilitating learning. Teachers, in turn, must be regarded as intelligent problem solvers, skillfully engaged in using themselves as instruments to bring about more efficient learning whether as individuals, as teams, schools or systems. Teachers must be valued as entrepreneurs, confronting the problems of student growth in a changing society and seeking creative solutions that contribute to the maximum fulfillment of those they are privileged to work with. To implement such an expanded view of the profession requires teachers who behave like true professionals. Like everyone else, the behavior of teachers is dependent upon how they see themselves, their goals and the situations in which they are engaged. Truly professional teachers are not cut from the same cloth. Instead, they are intelligent problem solvers, skilled at using themselves as instruments to facilitate the learning process. To do that well requires understanding of themselves, of students, subject matter, and the nature and purposes of society and its educational system. Good teachers have the capacity to put all these together in the unique mix required for maximal learning in their classrooms, laboratories or playing fields.

The Public Perception

On the larger scene, we need changes in public perception of the profession. This, of course, is not easy for public perceptions are not created simply by advertising or the provision of new information. The public belief about teaching is deeply ingrained in citizens from years of experience at the hands of traditional teachers. Personal experience always takes precedence over mere information or being told. Many citizens are also quite certain that the teachers they had and the ways they were taught are "the way it ought to be". "Look at me. That's how it was for me and I turned out just fine." Parents quickly grow anxious over innovations which they do not understand, especially if these depart from clear and rigorous pursuit of the basics. Time worn beliefs about teachers and the ways they should teach are further confirmed in the public view by the fact that many in the profession, itself, agree with such conceptions. Most teachers in the system still teach in ways little changed from a generation ago. This makes the problem of changing the public's conception of the teaching profession a difficult one. Despite the handicaps the effort for true professionalism must be made.

A demoralized profession cannot produce the person-centered, self renewing system required for real educational reform. We need to use our marvelous modern devices for communication to convey a new understanding of the profession, of its problems and the need for reform. Reports of modern research about learning and growth and new conceptions in educational thought and practice need wide dissemination. Public expectations that standardization, the industrial model and traditional ways of organizing, grouping and evaluating students are the way to go must be replaced with appreciation of the need for diversity and self renewing person-centered schools. Experiment and innovation must be the name of the game with local successes given the broadest possible circulation and encouragement.

A major handicap to the growth of true professionalism is the reciprocal fear of each other characteristic of parents and teachers. Most parents are afraid of teachers. They do not understand them, seldom have opportunities to interact with them, fear teacher evaluations of their children and are thrown into anxiety by the dreaded request for "a parent conference". Teachers and administrators, on the other hand, are equally fearful of parent disapproval and their control over school finances. Professional-public relationships are also exacerbated by parents and school boards who overstep the boundaries of policy and action and presume, not only to establish the goals and policies of education but, to tell the profession how to do it as well. This seriously undermines professionalism and should be resisted with the same firmness and dignity with which doctors, lawyers or engineers would respond to being told how to carry out their crafts.

Above all, teachers, themselves, need to act like professionals, projecting command of their jobs, pride in their accomplishments and expecting to be treated with the dignity and respect true professionalism deserves. Modern understanding about brain function, human growth and development, the dynamics of learning, individual and group behavior, curricula, to say nothing of the new needs of society and the future into which we are hurtling has made the practice of teaching a far cry from yesterday's models of "Ichabod Crane" or the "school marm". Teaching has become a highly skilled, professional occupation and it is time for teachers to insist upon the recognition and respect due the vital role they play in today's complex society. The growing strength of professional organizations in recent years is a long step in the right direction. The days of obsequious conformity are over. Educators at every level need to speak out about their profession, and band together to give force and substance to their emerging self respect.

A New Conception Of Good Teaching

Recent research tells us that good teaching is not simply a matter of knowledge of subject matter, although teachers certainly need to be well informed. Neither is good teaching the result of using right methods. Rather, research demonstrates that good teaching is a function of the teacher's personal system of beliefs; more precisely, beliefs about:

1. The primary data to focus on: Good teachers and administrators characteristically approach their tasks from an internal frame of reference. That is to say, they are people, rather than things oriented. They are empathic, continuously tuned in to how things seem to the persons they work with.

2. What people, including students, are like. Good practitioners typically see people in positive ways. They regard them as able, trustworthy persons of dignity and integrity. Poor teachers and administrators have serious doubts about their students and employees.

3. The teacher's self. Good teachers and administrators see themselves in essentially positive ways. They see themselves as liked, wanted,

acceptable, able, people of dignity and integrity. Poor ones see themselves in negative ways.

4. Purposes; society's, education's and the teacher's own. Good teacher's purposes for themselves, their students and society in general tend to be positive, socially constructive and personally fulfilling.

5. Appropriate personal methods. Good teachers have acquired a highly personal armamentarium of methods or ways of dealing with events that fit themselves, their students, the purposes of education, the curriculum and the circumstances within which they operate.

Whenever society or its institutions is confronted with a change in basic assumptions, vast changes are called for throughout the system. Just so, changes in our conception of the nature of learning and the teaching profession requires rethinking many goals and practices; with respect to student-teacher and teacher-administrator relationships, ways of teaching, the organization and administration of schools, teacher education and many more. For the teaching profession in particular, new understandings like those above call for major changes in at least the following areas:

1. In pre-service teacher preparation.
2. In in-service faculty development.
3. In the creation of facilitative atmospheres for the work place.

Pre-service Teacher Preparation

Traditional Programs

The production of true professionals begins with the teachers' colleges. To bring about and maintain the person-centered, self renewing schools we need for effective educational reform, requires thousands of teachers who are intelligent problem solvers, ready and able to cope effectively with the changing needs of modern education. As we have seen, people behave according to their beliefs or perceptions. More specifically, what makes a good teacher is the possession of a trustworthy set of beliefs, a kind of personal theory which determines a teacher's thinking and behavior on the job. If that is true, then the primary goal for teacher education must be the development of teacher belief systems that are comprehensive, accurate, internally consistent, personally relevant and adaptable to changing times and conditions. Unfortunately, few teachers' colleges are currently oriented toward such objectives.

Like the rest of education, the preparation of teachers has been dominated by manipulation of forces thinking. The task is defined as "teaching people how to teach". For at least three generations, most teachers' colleges in America have been predicated upon four basic assumptions----Good teachers need:

1. Mastery of subject matter: usually defined as a program of general studies plus specialization in one or more subject areas.

2. Understanding the "foundations of education"--- philosophy of education, growth and development of the learner, the nature of the learning process and the role of schools in society.

3. Appropriate methods for teaching subject matter specialties.

4. Supervised practice teaching----opportunity to practice under supervision what was learned in the above steps, generally placed at the end of the program.

Despite the long history of programs derived from these assumptions it is apparent that something is vitally wrong with the approach. They are not producing the kinds of professionals we need so desperately. Despite accreditation reviews, budget allocations, tougher selection measures, stricter supervision, increased requirements and longer time on task, the teachers we graduate continue to fall short of the expectations of laymen and professionals alike. The reason, it now seems clear, is that, the basic assumption which holds that good teaching is a consequence of knowledge and right behavior translated into the four assumptions above is only partly right. As we have seen earlier, partly right assumptions lead to partly right answers resulting in closed system solutions. Closed system thinking encourages us to continue trying harder in the same directions. The basic assumptions above have not changed in at least fifty years. It seems clear we are in need of new ones.

It has been a long time since teachers' colleges have made fundamental changes in basic assumptions. Meantime, the world has moved on leaving our present institutions vulnerable to attack from all sides. Even the teachers who come through the process are sharply critical of current programs. Follow up studies typically show that students regard their practice teaching experience as the primary contributor to their growth with all other aspects falling far behind. The assumptions upon which most current teacher preparation institutions are operating are inadequate to produce the true professionals required for today's world.

Inducing teachers colleges to change will not be easy for they, too, are caught up in a closed system of operation. The faculties of teachers colleges are typically trained in teachers' colleges and thoroughly indoctrinated in traditional assumptions. They seldom question the basic assumptions of the system. Even when they do, changes which question or depart from traditional assumptions are quickly shot down, if not by colleagues on the same faculty, then by existing accreditation agencies which generally look with disfavor upon departures from traditional assumptions. Reform in professional training requires breaking down these resistances. New assumptions derived from modern thinking and research are called for, followed by widespread experimentation and diversification of programs.

New Assumptions For Teacher Education

Perhaps the first assumption in need of change is the widespread notion that there are universal "right ways" to train teachers. This concept makes teachers colleges highly resistant to change. The nationally known teachers college from which I graduated more than fifty years ago is still essentially the same as when I was an undergraduate. From one end of the country to the other teachers colleges are remarkably alike monitored by national accreditation agencies proceeding from the same time worn assumptions

Like the rest of education, effective teacher preparation requires diversity. Teachers colleges ought not be carbon copies of one another any more than our public schools. Rather, each should express the thinking and activities of their respective faculties. Nor should diversity stop with differing colleges. Why not, a number of programs operating side by side within a college, each based upon a different set of assumptions or alternative ways of interpreting similar assumptions? Just as alternative schools are needed to speed reform in education generally, so, too, we need diversity and innovation in teacher preparation institutions.

It is not the intent of this book to prescribe the specific nature of teacher education programs. We have repeatedly made the point that there are no such things as right methods in education. Methods must fit local processes and conditions, the best information available and the faculties attempting to implement them. Reform in teacher education, must begin from careful examination of its basic assumptions followed by earnest attempts to implement new ones within the constraints of local conditions.

At least five basic principles from current psychological thought and research provide new foundations for the construction of more adequate teacher preparation programs. They are:

1. The causes of behavior lie in people's personal meanings or perceptions.

2. Learning must be understood as the personal discovery of meaning.

3. Learning is a deeply human process vitally influenced by need, the self concept, feelings of belonging, facilitative feedback and the dynamics of challenge and threat.

4. What makes a good teacher is the possession of a trustworthy system of personal beliefs to provide trustworthy on the job guidelines for effective thought and action.

5. There are no right methods. Instead, methods must fit the complicated nature of the person using them, the students, the curriculum and conditions confronted.

These well established facts about learning and behavior provide the foundations for new thought and practice in teacher education.

Sample Assumptions

A few teachers' colleges have attempted to translate such concepts into basic assumptions and then sought ways to implement them in policy and practice. Here, for example, are some samples drawn from the program designs of several institutions attempting to update their teacher education programs:

Assumption: <u>Teacher education must be seen as a process of personal becoming.</u>

Delineation: Other helping professions have preceded education in this respect. In medicine, for example, they do not say, "He is learning how to doctor". Rather, they say, "He is becoming a physician". In the legal field, the expression is not, "She is learning to law" but, "She is becoming a lawyer". Just so, teacher education must be seen, not as a matter of "learning how to teach" but as a process of <u>becoming a teacher</u>. An effective teacher education program must facilitate the development of personal belief systems that are dynamic, comprehensive, accurate, internally consistent and trustworthy.

Facilitative guidelines: 1. The program reflects sensitivity and empathy in its design and promotes interrelationships between students, between faculty and students and among the faculty itself.

132

2. Self direction requires student acceptance of responsibility for their own learning. Faculty has responsibility for providing experiences which facilitate making choices and taking personal responsibility.

3. Establishing seminars of thirty students each under supervision of an advisor-leader who is broadly knowledgeable about education and experienced in group dynamics. Seminars will include students at all levels and will engage students in continuous discussion of personal and professional matters in sessions meeting at least once per week. Students will be enrolled on entrance and remain throughout the program.

Assumption: People learn best when they have a need to know.

Delineation: The program should: a. seek maximum fulfillment of student needs,

b. Relate instruction to student needs,

c. Create needs to know prior to providing information.

Facilitative guidelines: 1. Field experience will be valued less as a place to practice teach, more as the place to discover what the problems of effective teaching are, (create needs to know). To this end, students will be actively involved in field experience throughout the program with increasing time in the classroom and increasing responsibility as they progress toward certification.

2. Instead of courses, subject matter will be offered in response to student needs. Faculty will seek to create needs to know before providing information.

3. All faculty specialists will be available to students throughout the program instead of only while students are enrolled in the specialist's course.

4. Procedures will be established to monitor student needs continuously and plan learning experiences accordingly. In one program this goal was implemented by having student representatives from each seminar meet with the faculty on Thursday of each week to plan the following week's content and experiences.

Assumption: Learning about methods must concentrate on the personal discovery of those appropriate for the teacher, students, subject matter and the circumstances under which they are used.

Facilitative guidelines: 1. The teaching of methods should occur cafeteria style--- through exposure to many possibilities and the encouragement of experimentation in order to discover what fits the individual teacher.

2. Provision of facilities to experiment with methods will be provided on campus, through a "curriculum lab", or simulation activities and off campus, by field experience.

Assumption: Effective feedback must be immediate, personal, related to the task and point the way to next steps.

Delineation: Grades violate all of the above criteria and should be eliminated from the program to be replaced by continuous constructive feedback.

Facilitative guidelines: 1. Feedback should be frequent and immediate as possible.

2. Feedback will be designed to identify strengths, competencies, skills, knowledge and point the way to further steps.

3. Evaluation is tailored to assess each student's individual progress and may take many forms; personal journals, exams, observations, critical feedback, seminar discussions, individual conferences, joint faculty-student evaluation of specific tasks, accumulation of a portfolio etc.

Assumption: The quality of student-faculty relationships is crucial.

Facilitative guidelines: 1. Despite lack of rigid regulations for everyone to follow, both students and faculty recognize interpersonal involvement as a top priority.

2. Students and faculty accept responsibility to be available to each other as needed.

3. Students should have close and continuing contacts with at least one faculty person throughout his/her participation in the program.

Assumption: Good teaching must be based upon the clearest, most accurate concepts available concerning the nature of persons and their behavior.

Facilitative guidelines: 1. The program will expose students to a variety of viewpoints in psychological thought, will provide opportunities to test such concepts against personal and professional experience.

2. The program will encourage the development of defensible personal beliefs about human behavior, personality, and the effective facilitation of student growth, development and learning.

Assumption: Good teachers see themselves in positive ways

Delineation: The program will facilitate views of self as able, worthy, acceptable, professional persons of dignity and integrity.

Guidelines: 1. faculty-student relationships will be designed to result in the above attitudes.

2. Classroom, laboratory and field experiences will foster positive feelings about self by treating students as though they were; able, worthy, acceptable, professional persons of dignity and integrity.

The assumptions and guidelines above are provided solely for illustration. The problem for teacher education is how to translate modern thought and practice into fundamental assumptions for teacher education. Different faculties will no doubt arrive at varying assumptions from the same fundamental data. That is the nature of human adaptability and will provide the kind of diversity in programs sorely needed at present. The crucial need is for engagement in the process of innovation. The sample assumptions above deal with matters most affected by modern research and learning theory. A truly effective teacher education program will, of course, need to include many additional concerns having to do with content, curricula, local problems and the nature of its faculty as well.

In-Service Programs

Most school systems recognize the need for in- service training of their faculties. For many, this consists of little more than requirements for the acquisition of college credits now and then. Other systems have elaborate in-service programs covering a wide variety of experiences both on and off campus. Much in-service activity, unfortunately, has little relevance for significant reform because it is formulated from traditional closed system thinking and rarely questions existing assumptions. Programs generally fall under one of four headings:

Inspirational programs: often at the beginning of the year. These usually consist of one or more speakers who may or may not have a significant message to deliver. Frequently they are more entertaining than profound.

Fund of knowledge programs: designed to increase the knowledge base of faculties, usually within the teacher's subject matter area. Faculty members may also be induced to seek further knowledge through obtaining additional college credits or attending workshops.

How-to programs: through which teachers may become acquainted with methods which have worked effectively somewhere. These are often taught in workshops led by local or imported experts. For teachers deeply ingrained with the idea that there are right methods, such programs are highly popular.

Action programs: aimed at finding solutions to local problems. These have great potential for innovation. Unhappily, more often than not, they are crisis or methods oriented; "What shall we do about drugs? Dropouts? Reading scores? Such programs are rarely concerned about basic assumptions or in depth solutions. Instead, the focus is almost exclusively centered upon coping.

Too often in-service programs are concerned with laid on solutions. They are instigated because someone, other than the participants, decided that; "We need an in-service program", "This is what we need to focus on" or "This is what they ought to work on". As a consequence programs begin with two strikes against them; lack of commitment and preoccupation with methods. Participants go through the motions of compliance and occasionally reap some personal benefit. As significant vehicles for reform, such programs rarely make it. Instead, they spin their wheels chasing after symptoms. To bring about serious reform, in-service programs must begin from committed involvement of participants, confront real problems, seek for broader understanding and lead to action directed at causes and basic assumptions rather than symptoms.

Facilitating Teacher Growth

Encouraging teachers to adopt and experiment with ideas is, itself, a learning experience unlikely to occur without the establishment of atmospheres which make innovation possible. Helping teachers to grow and discover new and better ways to teach is a learning process governed by the same principles that work for children. Just as modern principles must be applied in the classrooms, so too, they must guide administrators and supervisors to facilitate teacher growth and active participation in the search for better schools. Teachers, like students, must feel the need for change, discover the personal meaning of modern concepts about growth and learning and be actively involved in the search for better ways to teach and relate to students, the curriculum, colleagues and the system. They must see themselves as proud and capable professionals engaged in a continuous campaign to foster the growth of young people in the best, most efficient ways. They must feel encouraged and facilitated as individuals and as faculties.

First step toward the achievement of this happy condition calls for freeing teacher time for the investigation of ideas, communicating with colleagues, planning and experimentation with methods and curricula. Unfortunately, this obvious minimum requirement is usually negated by management and budgetary considerations which equate productivity with "contact hours" or FTE's (full time equivalents). Such viewpoints imply that teaching and learning only occur when teachers are engaged in face to face activities with students. Most public school teachers are hard pressed to find time to keep up with required reports, administrivia of a hundred varieties, paper grading or planning for next period. Time for exploration of ideas, meaningful communication with colleagues or participation in research and development projects, when it exists at all, is regarded as "discretionary" time subject to invasion for almost any reason. Time on task and contact hours are widely regarded as reliable indicators of effective learning and are made the basis of budget considerations, attendance requirements and teacher evaluations with no regard for the restraints they impose upon the possibilities for innovation and reform. Time spent for research and development is not wasted time, nor does it inevitably result in less effective teaching. My children attend a highly innovative laboratory school in which teachers are free to pursue whatever they need to every day from 7:30 to 9:00 A.M. when school starts and from 3:30 to 4:30 afternoons. They also have days off to visit other schools when needed and have had twelve "teacher planning days" this year (sans students) when the faculty works on all sorts of projects together. Everything I can observe demonstrates that my children and their classmates are getting a fine education.

Like pre-service programs, in-service efforts must concentrate on bringing about changes in the belief systems of participants. This requires dealing with real problems; not those that seem important to outsiders like supervisors and administrators, but those perceived as real by the in-service participants. Here in-service has a distinct advantage over teachers colleges which operate with inexperienced students and must create needs to learn. Teachers and administrators on the job are surrounded by problems and job success is often dependent upon solving them. Anyone who has ever had the experience of teaching teachers in courses on and off campus can attest to the difference in student attitudes. On campus, students are typically passive and write down everything instructors have to say because they do not have enough experience to discriminate between what is important and what is not. Teaching the same course in in-service is another matter. Teachers take fewer notes and are far more selective in listening, more active in discussion and more critical of the instructor.

Beyond Confrontation

Mere confrontation of problems is not enough to result in significant reform. Teachers and administrators deal with immediate problems every day on a "911" symptomatic level. The typical in-service scenario goes something like this:

1. "Well, look, we've got this problem. What shall we do about it?"

2. "Let's find out what others are doing about it."

3. Call in an expert. That information acquired, next step is;

4. "What shall we try?" So, something is tried. If it works everyone is content, the problem is solved. If not, it's back to the drawing board to try something else. Such trial and error procedures can help cope with a local problem but makes little or no contribution to real reform.

How people behave, we have seen, is only symptom. Measures aimed at changing behavior without reference to basic causes are purely symptomatic and temporary. In- service activities directed at solving immediate local problems can be a fruitful spawning ground for important reform efforts and valuable catalysts for the inception of person-centered programs and self renewing schools. To achieve that goal requires going beyond mere confrontation and management. Local problems have the advantage of seeming important and worth the investment of time and energy. Such commitment, in turn, can motivate a faculty to explore relevant assumptions, define new objectives, experiment with innovative techniques, develop new attitudes and relationships characteristic of truly professional and creative teams. In time, such teams can revamp the system and carry it to new frontiers of service and accomplishment.

Notes and References

General References:

Flinders, D. 1988. "Teacher isolation and the new reform" Journal of Curriculum and Supervision, 5, 17-29.

Gage, N. 1984. "What do we know about teacher effectiveness?" Phi Delta Kappan, 10,87-93.

Timar, T. and Kirp, D. 1989. "Educational reform in the 1980's. Lessons from the states". Phi Delta Kappan,15,504-511.

On public appreciation:

Ellena, W. et. al. 1961. Who's a good teacher? Washington, D.C., American Association of School Administrators, National Education Association.

Inman, V. 1984. "Certification of teachers lacking courses in education stirs battles in several states." Wall Street Journal, 6 January,39.

Lieberman,A. 1988. Building a professional culture in schools New York City, Teachers College Press.

National Education Association. 1987. The status of the American public school teacher, Washington, D.C., National Education Association.

Good teacher research:

See list of research reports in Notes and References, Chapter 5.

On new approaches to teacher education:

Combs, A. 1972. "Some basic concepts for teacher education", The Journal of Teacher Education, 23, 286- 290.

Combs, A. and Wass, H. 1974 Humanizing the education of teachers", Theory Into Practice, 13,123-129.

Combs, A. et. al. 1974. The professional education of teachers; A humanistic approach to teacher education, Boston, Allyn and Bacon.

Combs, A. et. al. 1974 <u>Humanistic teacher education: An experiment in systematic curriculum innovation</u>, Fort Collins, Co. Shields.

Combs, A. 1978. "Teacher education: The person in the process", <u>Educational Leadership</u>, 35, 558-563.

Combs, A. 1989. "New assumptions for teacher education" <u>Foreign Language Annals</u>, 22,129-135.

Roth, R. 1989. "The teacher education program: An endangered species", <u>Phi Delta Kappan</u>, 71, 319-323.

On in-service education:

ASCD 1990. <u>Changing school culture through staff development</u> 1990 Yearbook, Alexandria, Va. Association For Supervision and Curriculum Development.

Bacharach,S. et. al. 1987. "A career development framework for evaluating teachers as decision makers". <u>Journal of Personnel Evaluation In Education</u>, 1, 181- 194.

Joyce, B. et. al. "The self educating teacher: Empowering teachers through research" IN <u>Changing school culture through staff development</u> 1990 Yearbook, Washington, D.C., Association for Supervision and Curriculum Development.

McDonald, G.1989. "When outsiders try to change schools from the inside", <u>Phi Delta Kappan</u>,71,206-211.

CHAPTER 9

RESTRUCTURING THE SYSTEM

In this exploration of reform we have pointed to the need for: diversity, person-centered, alternative schools and programs, adaptation to new expectations from the social scene, incorporation of new conceptions of the learning process by a revitalized profession and a recommitment to action research. We have approached reform as the cumulative effect of thousands of grass roots professional solutions to educational problems. Our schools must no longer be regarded as a static system of interchangeable parts modeled after some grand design. Instead, we have called for a dynamic self renewing system. Schools and programs must become dynamic agents continually examining their fundamental assumptions and adapting to the needs of their constituents. This is not so much a reform as a revolution, a fundamental change in guiding philosophy from a closed system of thinking to a more open one. It calls for a basic shift from a things and power orientation to a person-centered system capable of continuous self renewal and maximum release of human potential.

To create such conditions will not be quick or easy. People do not readily change their long accustomed ways of thinking and behaving. Powerful vested interests also stand in the way. Custom and tradition, the fall out from generations of parental experience in traditional schools, a management oriented bureaucracy, inadequate professional training, large community investments in obsolete plants and facilities, to say nothing of lucrative markets for business and industry; all these present formidable obstacles to successful reform. It is comparatively easy to move from democratic to autocratic modes of operation. To move from closed to open systems of thinking is quite another matter. In the face of such odds, how shall we facilitate the change process? How can we encourage the establishment of the self renewing schools we so desperately need? The effort must be made; no matter what. To stick with the status quo commits the system to falling ever farther behind. Such a betrayal of our youth is unthinkable.

Previous chapters have dealt with goals and processes of reform and the need for a revitalized profession to bring it about. We have called for diversity and a system of self renewing schools, each built around a like minded faculty responsive to the nature of its students and the needs of its community. To achieve such a bottom up approach to reform will require important changes in the structure and administration of the system, especially in state and federal departments of education, local school boards and the roles and functions of administration.

State And National Bureaucracies

A significant development of the last thirty years has been the growth of national and state Departments of Education. These agencies have grown very rapidly as financial support for education has shifted from local property taxes to funding from state coffers. At first State Departments became involved in setting standards and preparing guidelines to assure that state appropriated funds were legitimately employed. As time passed legislative concern about education has resulted in the assignment of ever broader functions to state departments like, maintenance of standards, state wide testing programs, certification of teachers, the introduction and supervision of special programs, building and safety codes, special curriculum requirements and many more. The net effect of these acquisitions of function by state departments of education is to burden the system with further levels of bureaucracy, increased control over local school operations and accompanying restraints upon local planning.

On the National scene, the federal Department of Education has little direct control over local schools but, nevertheless, manages to exert an ever increasing influence through the strings attached to its deep pockets. As a consequence of research funding and stipends for special projects, it, too, wields an ever growing influence and many schools would be hard pressed if government funds were to be withdrawn. Ostensibly established to promote education, in fact, these governmental agencies often impede the processes of reform by usurping what ought to be the prerogatives of local control, by saddling the system with enormous amounts of busy work and imposing a top down approach to restructuring. Both state and national agencies are, almost exclusively, staffed by administrators deeply imbued with the manipulation of forces management philosophy and addicted to closed system thinking and action. The personnel who staff these agencies are mostly drawn to their jobs because they enjoy administration and the security of fringe benefits afforded by a government sinecure. Many become Department of Education administrators to escape from the stresses and strains of the classroom. For the most part, they are committed to manipulation of forces thinking. They value objectivity, statistics and research designs and deal with educational problems as numbers or computer print outs. Few are in close touch with those who directly interact with students at the front line of the profession.

Generally speaking, the state and national department approach to reform is through one or another variety of laid on solutions. These are more concerned with maintenance of the system, how things are, than enhancement of the system, how schools ought to be. Even the thrust of research and development grants gets blunted by self fulfilling loops that reward proposals designed to do more of the same. Applications for research or innovation grants, for example, are typically submitted to "experts" in the field for review and recommendation. These "experts", of course, are folks who have made a name for themselves in the system. They are understandably loathe to endorse revolution. When you have spent thirty years of your life advocating a way of thinking or acting, it is hard to applaud the proposal of some newcomer who threatens to demonstrate how wrong you were. Everything about the nature and function of state and federal bureaucracies conspires to make them unlikely agents for major change. They tolerate innovation within traditional assumptions but tend to reject major departures from the status quo.

To create the atmospheres we need for bottom up restructuring and self renewal, it will be necessary to reduce State and National Department control over public schools. Effective reform requires diversity of program, alternative schools, and atmospheres that encourage risk taking and innovation. Unhappily, these are more impeded than fostered by government agencies. A new breed of government employees who are familiar with the person- centered thinking required for open system approaches to innovation and reform is required. We are not likely to get them, however. State and national department employees are generally appointed or selected by those already on board, a device which practically guarantees maintenance of the status quo. It is asking too much that state and national offices become risk taking change agents and they are too far removed from the locus of critical action. We had better look elsewhere for reform leadership while encouraging state and federal departments of education to confine their activities to statistical and support functions or to precisely defined tasks which do not interfere with grass roots experiment and innovation.

School Boards And The Public

To bring about the restructuring required for effective reform will require tackling the problem of change at every level. The general public needs much broader understanding of the reform problem. Too many citizens see the task in simplistic terms of management and control instead of the fundamental restructuring required by changing societal expectations on one hand, and new understanding about learning and growth on the other. A major effort is called for to help citizens understand the true scope of the problem and the new assumptions required. An informed public can help create a facilitating atmosphere for change. It would be a great pity if the current public outcry for change was permitted to blow itself out for lack of concentration upon truly vital issues. A public dialogue around the values and assumptions which must form the basis for action is desperately needed.

A major effort is required from the media and the profession to move the locus of public discussion from management, things and traditional expectations to more basic considerations. Simplistic thinking and reliance upon past experience is no longer enough. The changing demands of American society, the global world we must cope with and the future for which we are preparing our youth are setting new goals for our schools. At the same time new discoveries about human behavior and the learning process require new thinking about the ways we teach and the nature of the institutions we design. To create a more promising atmosphere for reform, the public, which sets the goals and pays the bills, must be made aware of these new developments. To that end, we need a more aggressive, revitalized profession speaking out on educational issues. Full use of the media and the marvels of communication technology must be employed to provide citizens with new information and a nationwide forum for dialogue.

The School Board Role

The United States is the only country to vest primary control of its schools in local school boards. One would think that such an arrangement would result in great diversity in America's schools. The result is quite the opposite. It has produced schools remarkably similar from one end of the country to the other. There are many reasons for this. Most school boards are composed of part time, unpaid citizens and very few are in close touch with modern educational thought and practice. School board members seek to protect the interests of their constituents who, like school board members, themselves, look to their own school experience to judge what ought to be. Over the years, with the growth of larger and larger schools, school boards have lost the close relationships with schools and faculties they once had. Many now oversee the operations of numerous schools, thousands of students, even a number of diverse communities. Once school boards were composed of parents or citizens interested in the local school. Today, more often than not, they are political entities. Many are as far out of touch with students and teachers as the Board of Directors of a large corporation is with the corporation's individual employees. Such school boards are a far cry from the relationships required to establish and facilitate the self renewing, person- centered schools we currently need.

Close association between school boards and their schools has been seriously eroded by the nationwide movement toward larger and larger systems. They must, therefore, depend very heavily upon the superintendent, who walks a tightrope between maintaining majority support from the board on one hand, and managing the system on the other. Since superintendents are primarily managers, rather than educators, most operate from the traditional manipulation of forces approach and the time honored industrial model. Superintendents look to familiar management assumptions and the practices of "well run" schools as models to emulate. Their jobs are more dependent upon keeping people content than running the risks of innovation. Hence, the guidance they provide their school boards tends to maintain the status quo.

Creating Atmospheres For Change

Person-centered schools must be in close touch
with the citizens and communities they serve. To that end, every school needs its own school board or advisory committee composed of citizens interested in education and representative of the local community's goals and resources. Such an arrangement would be an important step toward reversing the trend to bigness and remote control which has exacerbated current problems of reform. Close relationships between school boards and school faculties will make dialogue more likely as school boards express the needs of the community and provide support for the school. Faculties, for their part, will have improved opportunity to be involved in decision making, keep community expectations in closer line with reality, acquaint the board and community about professional matters and have improved access to community attention to the needs of students and the profession.

A major drawback to conducive atmospheres for innovation lies in the confusion of many school boards over responsibility for policy and action. It is the responsibility of the board to inform the profession about what the community expects of its schools and to provide the support required to carry out those objectives. Professional educators, on the other hand, have responsibility for implementing policy and are presumed to have the training and experience to do so. Restructuring can be seriously inhibited or destroyed altogether by school boards who attempt to dictate or control the ways in which teachers and administrators carry our their functions. The very essence of a viable profession lies in freedom to confront and solve problems intelligently in the light of the practitioner's knowledge and experience. We do not tell surgeons how to perform an operation or engineers how to construct a bridge or lawyers how to plead a case. Neither should school boards presume to tell the teaching profession how to teach. When prescribed solutions are mandated by school boards or administrators, the profession is emasculated and reduced to automatons. Failure to understand this point undermines the morale of the profession and is an important contributor to its current low level of self esteem. School boards need to tell the profession what the community wants, provide the means to facilitate its achievement, then hold the profession responsible for accomplishing reasonable objectives. How the task is accomplished must be the unimpeded prerogative of the profession. The self renewing schools we need can only be achieved by a committed profession willing to tackle problems and free to exert its expertise with a minimum of interference.

The kind of thinking we have advocated in this volume will surely be seen by many school boards as frighteningly progressive, liberal, permissive or worse. Some progress can be made despite such drawbacks because current school board members are often remote from the scene of action and rely heavily upon superintendents for guidance. Much more can be accomplished with a board in close touch with a single school and its faculty, that has done its homework, has some depth of understanding about the issues involved and awareness of basic assumptions. They can also exert major influence by the quality of leadership they hire and the expectations they define for the superintendent.

Person-centered Leadership

We have advocated a bottom up approach to reform calling for diversity throughout the system with action research, alternative schools or programs and reliance upon an entrepreneurial profession as necessities for educational renewal. How well we achieve that end will be dependent upon the kinds of atmospheres created within the system. Professional morale, action research and self renewal require a climate of trust and respect, where risk taking is encouraged and people are regarded as more important than things. Unfortunately, the present administrative structure of our public schools is ill equipped to meet those criteria. In the present scheme of things the introduction of new assumptions into the system runs head on into prevailing philosophy and practice of much of school administration. School management has grown top heavy and operates, for the most part, from a basic philosophy that tends to stifle reform.

It is a matter of wonder to foreign educators visiting our schools to observe the numbers of administrators characteristic of American education. Many an elementary school in Great Britain, for example, operates efficiently with no more than a "head teacher" in charge who may spend a significant portion of his/her time as a classroom teacher as well. In contrast, we have the most prolific school bureaucracy of any nation in the world. Even in 1960 Martin Mayer found more administrators in New York City than the entire country of France and more in New York State than in all of Western Europe! (Mayer,1961) Since then, the situation has grown much worse. Our system is overloaded with administrators, in large part an outcome of the manipulation of forces, management thinking characteristic of industry in the

60's and 70's.

Because the prestige of administrators is directly proportional to the numbers of persons they administer, their numbers keep growing. So do the rules, regulations, guidelines, surveys, statistics and policy memos laid upon teachers along with oceans of paper work designed to make sure of proper compliance. Despite this excess baggage, there is little evidence to show that the system is more efficient or student achievement is markedly improved. For too many of education's leaders managing the system has taken precedence over facilitating the learning and growth of students. Meanwhile, the costs of administration continue to rise siphoning badly needed funds from classrooms, faculty selection and support or research and development activities. Any effort to redress this maldistribution of energies is bound to run into stiff resistance for administrators are in the driver's seat. They hold the reins and wield the power to facilitate or retard the processes of renewal.

Leadership For Reform

Achieving the self renewing, person-centered schools we need calls for a different kind of leadership. Changes are especially needed in three areas; 1. Basic thinking and philosophy, 2. The personal qualities of administrators and 3. New knowledge and skill requirements.

1. Basic Thinking or Philosophy

The People Problem

A major contributor to the bogged down condition of current education and to the failure of so many valiant efforts at reform lies in the "things" orientation which has so preoccupied the system for several generations. We have approached the problems of education at every level as matters to be dealt with by the manipulation of things. In the classroom we have approached learning from a behavioristic frame of reference dependent upon the application of stimuli, reward and punishment, telling and testing. In teacher education manipulation of forces thinking has treated teacher preparation as a mechanical process restricted to curriculum and methods. In leadership and administration it has taken the form of management, the manipulation of things and people to achieve desired ends. But education is a people problem and a things orientation is bound to be inadequate and frustrating. The leadership required to bring about the self renewing, person-centered schools we need must begin from a more humane set of basic assumptions. It must define its problem as changing people, arm itself for the task with the best information available about how people grow, learn and change and then facilitate those processes in the teachers who operate at the front lines of education. Effective reform requires supervisors, administrators and curriculum leaders skilled at facilitating change in teachers and administrators at the front lines of the education process. It calls for persons who understand and relate well to people, who know how to create challenging, unthreatening atmospheres, who understand, among other things, open systems for problem solving, the dynamics of group process and action research. Unfortunately, few administrators meet those criteria. Most current administrators are trained and experienced in closed system thinking, selected for management skills and operate from a manipulation of forces strategy. Too many administrators are things, rather than people oriented and many do not even believe person-centered skills are relevant to their tasks.

Open System Thinking

A second major shift in general strategy requires a change from closed to open systems of thinking and acting. As we have seen, closed systems work fine with things but tend to break down when applied to persons. If education and reform is a people problem, a system of thinking especially designed for human problems is essential. That calls for open system approaches, empathic understanding of teachers and students and facilitative skills aimed at helping people change from within. For persons deeply ingrained in closed system thinking the shift to open systems will be difficult and painful. The move from closed to open systems of thinking is always much slower and more difficult than the other way round. Newcomers to open system thinking must overcome long years of experience, training and habits so in grown as to be "second nature". Despite the best of intentions, deeply ingrained habits of thinking and acting are hard to shake. Example: the present movement toward greater autonomy in individual schools is still called "site based management" betraying the fundamental philosophy. Although the leash is extended, the locus of authority remains in the hands of traditional administrators. Permitting a school to make more of its own decisions is one thing, freeing it to become a truly alternative school is quite another.

The basic shift from closed to open thinking in administration parallels the shift in teaching from a manipulation of forces concept to a person-centered view of learning. Teachers are further along in this process than administrators, however, for a number of reasons. For one thing, they are closer to their consumers and, especially at elementary levels, are more person oriented. They are in intimate contact with students and so, are exposed to immediate feedback in their relationships. Increasing numbers of teachers have discovered person-centered thinking and are beginning to try out its implications for the classroom. Helping administrators to a comparable shift will be much more difficult. Closed system thinking is more deeply entrenched and one way, top down communication cuts managers off from consumer feedback that might help them see the need for change. If you don't hear from people, it is easy to assume that everything is going along just fine so there is little need to change. The higher up the organization ladder, the more administrators are isolated from the need to question their assumptions.

To achieve and operate the person-centered, self renewing schools we have advocated requires a distinct shift in the nature and functions of school administration. A system seeking reform from the bottom up needs leaders who are facilitators rather than managers, who understand and are skilled in open system thought and action. Such a change in philosophy and concept for administration is revolutionary. It calls for changes in basic assumptions and threatens long standing traditions, practices and privileges. As such it is bound to be strenuously resisted. It may even be too much to ask for its widespread adoption in the near future. We may have to wait for traditional practitioners to retire before open systems can make a significant entrance into common thought and action.

2. Some Personal Qualities of Leadership.

In previous chapters we have alluded several times to a series of researches on good and poor practitioners in the helping professions (see chapters 5 and 6). To implement the reforms needed for self renewing, person- centered, alternative schools calls for people oriented helpers of the highest quality. According to the research findings this means they will need:

To be sensitive human beings, continually tuned in to how things seem from the points of view of the persons they work with.

To be person, rather than things, oriented.

To see themselves in positive ways. To see those they work with as able, friendly, trustworthy persons of dignity and integrity.

To be authentic, self revealing persons.

In addition, they will need to possess comprehensive, accurate and internally consistent personal value or belief systems to provide trustworthy guidelines for thought and action including accurate understanding of themselves, of society, education and the future for which they are preparing youth. Furthermore, because the world is so rapidly changing, they must be life long learners, continuously engaged in keeping themselves up to date.

3. The Skills of Person-centered Administration.

Self renewing, person-centered schools and programs require like minded faculty groups committed to soundly based assumptions and given the freedom to experiment in search of the most effective ways to implement them. To bring such plans to fruition calls for person-centered leaders skilled in the creation of atmospheres conducive to innovation, who know how to stimulate ideas and facilitate faculty interaction. At the very least, facilitative leaders will need such understanding and skills as:

In depth understanding of human motivation and behavior,

Understanding of and expertise at facilitating communication,

In depth understanding of the learning process and its implemention,

Understanding of group process and skill in the facilitation of team projects,

Counseling skills,

Understanding of the dynamics of change,

In depth knowledge of community needs and resources,

Clear perceptions of the goals and purposes of education, teaching and curriculum,

Keen awareness of the future and its demands.

Such a person oriented list of qualifications is a far cry from the training and experience of most currently employed administrators. Compare the topics above, for example, with the following list of required courses for MA and PhD degrees in school administration extracted from the catalogue of a major teachers college.

MA Level:

Governance of American Education
School Finance and Budgeting
Law and the Administrator
Planning and Change in Education
School Personnel Administration
The School Principalship

Foundations of Curriculum Development and Instructional Practice.
Introduction to Graduate Research

Doctoral level:

Policy Analysis and Development
Seminar on Organization and Administration Theory
Seminar on Executive Leadership
Internship in Educational Administration
Practicum on Management of Change
Analysis of Variance
Evaluation Models and Design
Advanced Research Methods
Doctoral Proposal Research
Doctoral Dissertation

Some Signs of Change

Fortunately the winds of change are beginning to be felt among administrators here and there. Many administrators are delightful, hard working persons, honestly concerned about students and learning. Increasing numbers are becoming disenchanted with traditional closed system concepts of leadership and are becoming aware that traditional patterns need change. There is, for example a growing movement toward greater diversity and autonomy of action at the individual school level expressed in "site based" and "schools of choice" proposals. There is also a trend among forward looking administrators to value "emergent" forms of leadership similar in many ways to the open systems thinking we have reviewed in Chapter five.

The shift in thinking about leadership from a things oriented, authority and management concept toward a more person-centered frame of reference is barely getting under way in education. It is an ironic twist that the industrial model cherished for so long by educational administrators is, itself, undergoing rapid change as industry leans more and more to smaller autonomous units, employee control over tasks, facilitation of two way communication and grass roots participation in decision making. Similar trends in education toward a more person-centered, facilitative role is a commendable effort and needs to be given every possible support and encouragement.

The leadership changes required are not matters that can be simply defined and easily taught or learned. The shift from closed to open thinking, from management to facilitation is not a surface or methodological change. It is a fundamental reordering of personal values and beliefs. Person-centeredness cannot be successfully "acted" or put on or off like a suit of clothes. It represents a new way of seeing one's self and the world, a kind of personal theory providing guidelines for thinking and acting. It is a way of being and behaving that permeates an individual's public and private activities.

There is no universal job description for person-centered leaders any more than there is one for teachers. Effective leaders, like effective teachers, are persons who have acquired a comprehensive, accurate and internally congruent set of personal beliefs. Effective person-centered leadership is a matter of personal discovery, of learning how to use one's self to facilitate the growth and activities of others. Accordingly, the observations we have made about helping teachers to become person-centered agents of change, apply as well for educational leaders whether at the level of in-service education or training programs in the colleges.

Moving The System

The problem of bringing about a more person-centered style of leadership to speed reform is fraught with difficulty. Perhaps the move toward site based, person-centered alternative schools will help reduce the overall numbers of administrators. That may serve to lessen opposition to open system thinking somewhat but still leaves a long way to go. People do not change readily, especially when asked to make fundamental changes in long established ways of thinking. To speed the processes of reform it may be necessary to separate the business aspects of administration from person-centered functions. Every school activity involves matters most effectively dealt with by closed system, management approaches. Unfortunately, a good many practicing administrators get seduced by the concrete character of business matters. There are readily observable consequences when you deal with things and one can point with pride to "I did that". What's more things solutions generally stay done. Dealing with people is far more complex and one is never quite certain that "I did it" or that other people will know who did it. It is easy, therefore, for administrators to spend ever increasing proportions of their time upon the concrete, practical aspects of their jobs and to neglect the human, facilitative phases of leadership. The matter is complicated by the difficulties imposed by wearing two hats.

Being the boss and being a successful facilitator are often mutually exclusive. Many circumstances call for direct or immediate action and there is personal satisfaction in wielding power and "making things happen". It is an easy thing, therefore, for leaders to become preoccupied with management and addicted to closed system thinking. This preoccupation, in turn, causes the persons they work with to react in ways that only perpetuates the boss-employee relationship. People expect bosses to provide the answers and directions. This inhibits the acceptance of personal responsibility or commitment and results in an attitude of "It's the boss's problem, Let him/her solve it". The facilitator role is inconsistent with authority. Because it takes time to be a facilitator (open system) but easy to be an authority (closed system), many administrators slide into the authority role and never come out again.

It is so difficult and time consuming to go from the management to the facilitative role that clear separation of the two functions may prove to be the better option. Accordingly, a person-centered elementary school might be led by a principal selected for facilitative skills, assisted by a secretary, coordinator or manager responsible for business, maintenance and record keeping affairs. Alternatively, a school might be organized with a principal responsible for business affairs and one or more faculty persons responsible for human relationships, curriculum and school development or professional functions.

The problem of obtaining the leadership required to bring about the reforms advocated in this volume is far too big and complex to be adequately dealt with here. It is one thing to ask administrators and supervisors to change the teachers they supervise and manage; it is quite another to ask them to change themselves. It is especially difficult when the changes required are not mere ways of behaving but revision of long established ways of thinking and believing about themselves, their jobs, relationships and fundamental ways of working. We have argued that reform in education must be tackled from the bottom up through the involvement of participants in action research, critical analysis of basic assumptions, the adoption of new, more adequate ones and the support and facilitation of innovation and experimentation throughout the system. Those principles apply to up dating the leadership of education as well.

In Conclusion

The task of reforming American education is enormous. We have allowed ourselves to slip far out of touch with the needs of society and the demands of the future for which we are preparing our youth. Neither have we adapted the system to the advances of scientific discovery. The task of recovery is great and the hour is late. Almost everyone has something to suggest for our salvation. Most of these are simplistic notions based upon outmoded manipulation of forces assumptions and distract us from taking a hard look at our fundamental beliefs about education and learning. Meanwhile the system drifts deeper and deeper into the doldrums and increasingly fails our young people.

To reduce the chasm which currently exists between daily practice and the best we know about the learning process requires that teachers and administrators become keenly aware of new understandings about learning and encouraged to implement them in all aspects of their interactions with teachers and students. If modern principles were fully applied in classrooms we would quickly find ourselves with very different kinds of schools, more responsible student bodies and a long way on the road to the restructured, self renewing schools we need.

We are fortunate that over the past thirty years modern science has discovered a whole series of new understandings about human learning and growth. These have vast implications for all aspects of education. They represent exciting breakthroughs in biological and social science of conceivably greater import than the breakthroughs of physical science we have come to take so for granted. I have based this book upon some of those findings and suggested we update our system by replacing old assumptions with newer. more accurate ones. I have also presumed to suggest some directions such new thinking might take us. I have proposed no simple answers but have acquired a deep respect for the enormity of the problem we face and a firm sense of hope and excitement about where new thinking can lead.

I feel sure that some will read these pages in frustration because they contain no clearly defined "how to" prescriptions. I would like some of those too. But education is a people business and people do not change easily. Neither do they respond constructively to coercion and laid on solutions. Our founding forefathers established the principle that "when people are free, they can find their own best ways". In that spirit I think we can best approach the problems of educational reform by inducing the profession to examine its fundamental assumptions and replace them with new and better ones. I have worked very closely with educators all my professional life and I have discovered that when they are treated as responsible professionals, are given the time and freedom to think and experiment, they come up with far better answers than anything I, as an outsider, can usually suggest. That road to reform seems slower, it is true; I am convinced it is also more certain and effective in the long run.

155

Notes and References

General References:

LePage, A. 1987. <u>Transforming Education</u> Oakland, Ca. Oakmore House Press.

Nash, P. 1980. "The future of schooling" <u>Journal Of Thought</u> 15,17-25.

Schlesinger, A. 1986. "The challenge of change" <u>New York Times Magazine</u> July 27:20-21.

On leadership:

Bennis, W. 1978. <u>The unconscious conspiracy: Why leaders can't lead</u> New York, Amacone.

Combs, A.W. 1970. "The human aspect of administration." <u>Colorado Journal of Educational Research</u>, 9, 9-15.

Leiberman, A. and Miller, L. 1986. "School improvement: Themes and variations" IN Leiberman, A. <u>Rethinking school improvement</u> New York, Teachers College Press.

Raywid, M. 1989. "Restructuring school governance: Two models" Unpublished paper. Hempstead, N.Y., Hofstra University.

On Current Administration

Chubb, J. and Moe, T. 1990. <u>Politics, markets and American schools</u>. Washington, D.C., Brookings Institution.

Kearns, D. 1988. "An educational recovery plan for America". <u>Phi Delta Kappan</u> 45,565-570.

Mayer, M. 1961. <u>The school</u> New York, Harper and Row.

Rollis,S. and Highsmith,M. 1986. "The myth of the great principal: Questions of school management and instructional leadership". <u>Phi Delta Kappan</u>, 68, 300- 304.

Shanker,A. 1990. <u>Staff development and the restructured school</u>. Alexandria, Va. Association for Supervision and Curriculum Development.

Moving the system:

Educational Commission of the States, 1988. "Re: Learning principles for changing the education system". Denver, Co. Educational Commission of the States.

Elmore, R. 1986. Models of restructured schools Stanford, Ca. Center for Policy Research in Education.

Harvey,G. and Crandall, D. 1988. A beginning look at the what and how of restructuring Andover, Ma. Regional Laboratory for Educational Improvement of the New England Schools.

Hennes, J. 1989 Restructuring education: strategic options required for excellence. Denver, Co. Colorado Department of Education.

Howard, E. and Griffin, T. 1986. A school for the 80's and 90's: A priority search for schools and school clusters. Denver, Co. Colorado Department Of Education.

Joyce, B. et. al. 1989. "School renewal as cultural change." Educational Leadership, 47,70-77.

Olson, L. 1988. "The restructuring puzzle". Education Week Nov. 2. 7-11.

Timor, T. 1989. "The politics of school restructuring". Phi Delta Kappan 71,264-275.

Vickery, T. 1988. "Learning from an outcomes driven school district". Educational Leadership 45, 52-57.

APPENDIX

CHECKLIST FOR HUMANISTIC SCHOOLS

Doris M. Brown, Task Force Chairman,

ASCD Working Group On Humanistic Education

1978

Items are listed in rank order as arranged by
Educators, teachers and high school students

1. Teachers who are genuine, warm and empathic.
2. Student mistakes not resulting in damaged self concept.
3. Policies aimed directly at maintaining personal worth, dignity and rights of students.
4. Staff treating students with same courtesy and respect accorded peers.
5. Students listening to each other.
6. Necessary discipline treatment tempered with compassion and understanding.
7. Staff emphasizing positive rather than negative consequences in guiding behavior.
8. A library with an abundance of books and other materials.
9. Principal truly using the staff and students in making decisions which affect them.
10. Teachers conveying through action that they trust the students.
11. At least once a day, teachers finding the time and incident to indicate to each student," I care who you are".
12. Activities which encourage divergent thinking and other forms of creative effort.
13. Teachers using objectives for humane teaching rather than against it; pacing, teacher time management for greater individual attention, student choice.
14. Teachers showing competence in subject matter content.
15. Developmental characteristics of students taken into consideration more than age and grade when planning learning experiences.
16. Staff able to detect and respond appropriately to signs of personal problems of students.
17. Free access to counselors, nurses, tutors and other special personnel.
18. Teachers making verbal or non verbal responses to students to indicate, "I hear you".
19. All students receive some "ego builders", honors, status, roles, "happy grams", positive comments by others.
20. Teachers giving observations as feedback, not judgement.
21. Small group field trips and excursions which make in-school learning relevant.
22. Students readily assisting and sharing with other students.
23. Students involved in discovery and "hands on" activities.
24. A school philosophy, including values and attitude concerns, being used by teachers in planning classroom activities.
25. Free discussion of questions and issues not covered in the text.
26. Teachers motivating students with intrinsic value of ideas or activity.
27. Teachers having greater concern for the person involved than for task achievement.
28. Curriculum materials accurately reflecting our multi-ethnic society and varying family structures.

29. Evidence of well planned lessons.

30. Access to activities regardless of sex, age, personality or other characteristics.

31. Interest or learning centers being used with purpose.

32. Students talking enthusiastically about what they are doing in school.

33. Teachers making comments during a dialogue with students,i.e. "tell me more", "that sounds interesting".

34. New students and family members given a tour of the building and an explanation of the program.

35. A student attitude of, "I've chosen this hard thing. Learning is challenging, stretching, sometimes hard, but Oh so worth it!"

36. Wide variety of courses and special events from which to choose.

37. Staff seeking training in communications and human relations.

38. Evaluation of student work emphasizing correct response instead of errors.

39. Planned school interactions which foster appreciation of human differences.

40. Students questioning accuracy, applicability and appropriateness of information.

41. Spontaneous discussion being encouraged.

42. Principals and teachers seeking suggestions from parents.

43. An entrance area with a friendly decor which displays students work.

44. Students involved in self evaluation.

45. Students, teachers and parents displaying symbols of school pride.

46. Students sharing classroom and school responsibilities.

47. Teachers knowing specific things each student likes and dislikes as well as personal
tragedies and successes.

48. Adults laughing with students; lots of smiling.

49. Learning organized around student's own problems or questions.

50. Community volunteers assisting in learning centers, libraries, teaching technical skills and serving as special resources.

51. Opportunities for students to be involved in career exploration or job location through out of school work.

52. A resource center in which students are free to use projectors, filmstrip viewers and cassette tape recorders.

53. Teachers who view teaching as one of "freeing" rather than controlling.

54. Class meetings held to discuss solutions to problems which arise.

55. Space outside where people can run.

56. Teachers seeking parent evaluation of child's progress.

57. Student records which note student's strengths and interests more than limitations.

58. Playground with grass as well as asphalt.

59. Teacher stopping to talk to parents in the school.

160

60. Teachers questioning misconceptions, faulty logic and unwarranted conclusions.
61. Teachers working, playing, learning along with students.
62. Evaluations as important in areas of personal-social development as in academic progress.
63. Spontaneous laughter.
64. Representative student governments dealing with relevant school problems.
65. Utilization of available non-classroom space for activities, i.e. learning centers, tutoring.
66. Teachers building student ideas into the curriculum.
67. Teacher disclosing aspects of own experience relevant to the teaching-learning.
68. System for students accepting responsibility for movement within the school and to other places of learning.
69. Outsiders feeling welcome in the classroom.
70. Working outdoors when it is appropriate to the experience.
71. Student access to materials for on-going projects.
72. Principal spending some of his/her time working with students.
73. Space to "move around" in every classroom.
74. Availability of tools and scientific instruments for use by students.
75. Staff and students sharing resources.
76. Student sub-groupings based on special interests, social preference, as well as skill needs.
77. Parents welcomed as members of the instructional team.
78. Classwork evolved from out of school events in the lives of students.
79. A brief period each day to do "fun things".
80. Teacher talk supplemented with some friendly gestures.
81. Alternatives to traditional grading systems.
82. "I'll help with that" actions by teachers.
83. Students working independently on what concerns them.
84. Secretary providing a positive greeting when meeting visitors, students and faculty.
85. Human development and the study of humanity a regular part of the curriculum.
86. Teachers not expecting student to come up with the answer he/she has in mind.
87. Absence of negative comments to students by teachers.
88. Students working independently in small groups.
89. Teachers greeting students entering or leaving classrooms.
90. A setting for student dramatic and musical productions.
91. Students having time to sit, think and mull things over.
92. All students evaluating the classroom and school instructional program.
93. Senior citizens involved with students, at school, in their homes and in

care homes.
94. Students doing some of the teaching and other leadership tasks
95. Student task-oriented committees.
96. Students able to go to the school resource center whenever needed.
97. Teachers spending some of their unscheduled time with students.
98. Libraries, laboratories, shops and recreational areas available to students after school hours.
99. Surprise exhibits such as a litter of pups, white rabbits, unusual type plants.
100. Students engaged in community service.

INDEX

164

166

ABOUT THE AUTHOR

Arthur Combs began his teaching career in the public schools of Alliance, Ohio in 1935. To improve his skills in helping students, he sought a doctorate in Clinical Psychology at Ohio State and spent the next ten years operating a psychological clinic and training students in counseling and psychotherapy at Syracuse University. During this period he developed the conviction that therapy is essentially rehabilitative and the more important task lies in prevention---helping people before they get sick. This concern led him back to education and he accepted a position at the University of Florida in 1951. In the years following he was, at various times, Professor of Education, Chairman of the Foundations in Education Department and Director of the Center For Humanistic Education. In 1975 he left Florida to devote full time to writing, consulting in education and psychology and the private practice of psychotherapy.

He returned to academia for a five year period in the 80's as Distinguished Professor at the University of Northern Colorado. His most recent interests lie in contributing to the educational reform movement through writing, consulting and occasional teaching. He is also engaged in the private practice of psychotherapy with Community Counseling Associates, 2525 Sixteenth St., Greeley, Colorado. 80631.

Dr. Combs considers himself both a product of and a contributor to the Humanist Movements in psychology and education. With Donald Snygg in 1947, he invented perceptual-experiential psychology, a systematic frame of reference for the study of persons. Most of his career since then has been devoted to the applications of perceptual-experiential thinking to research and practice in education, counseling and the training of persons for the helping professions.

He is a past president of the Association For Supervision and Curriculum Development and a recipient of the John Dewey Award for Distinguished Service to Contemporary Education. Speaking and consulting appearances have taken him to every state and to seven foreign countries. His writings include twenty two books and monographs and more than one hundred fifty articles on psychology, counseling and education. His works have been translated into Spanish, German, Dutch, Portuguese, Hebrew, Korean and Japanese.